Sacrament of Service

Sacrament of Service

A Vision of the
Permanent Diaconate Today

by
Rev. Patrick McCaslin

and
Michael G. Lawler

PAULIST PRESS
New York/Mahwah

Library of Congress
Catalog Card Number: 85-62874

ISBN: 0-8091-2758-X

Published by Paulist Press
997 Macarthur Boulevard
Mahwah, New Jersey 07430

Printed and bound in the
United States of America

Contents

DEDICATION

To the Men and Women of the Diaconate Community
of the Archdiocese of Omaha
Who are teaching us the meaning of this Sacrament

Introduction

*F*or quite some time we have had the need to write about the experience of the last fourteen years of living with the permanent diaconate. "Living" has included for one of us, Fr. Patrick McCaslin, a priest of the archdiocese of Omaha, being director of the diaconate program in that diocese, giving retreats around the nation to various other diaconate groups, and being intimately involved on the national level as the first president of the National Association of Permanent Diaconate Directors (NAPDD). It has included for the other, Dr. Michael Lawler, professor of theology at Creighton University in Omaha, being a principal educator and resource person in the Omaha program and a speaker and consultant for other programs around the country. Since we have worked together in the formation of deacons since 1971, it seemed to us that our broad experience and insight could come together in an extended reflection on the diaconate. The result is this book in which we have attempted to set forth our understanding of the essence of the permanent diaconate in the hope that others would come to our deep appreciation of this renewed order in the Church, and indeed of the Church itself. How well we have succeeded must be left, of course, to the judgment of the reader.

It has long been our concern that any search for the meaning of the diaconate should concentrate on three areas: (1) the humanity of Jesus; (2) the nature of the Church; (3) the Catholic notion of sacramentality. We have attempted to pursue that concentration in this book, hoping to show that any practical conclusions about the diaconate should be derived from sound theological bases, and not just from the functional pragmatism we hear all around us today. By functional pragmatism we mean statements such as: "Any lay person can do anything a deacon can do, so why ordain deacons?" As a statement about a functionary, that statement can get by; but as a statement about a

3

sacrament, which we believe and shall argue that a deacon is, it makes as much theological sense as the statement that pouring water on people makes them nothing but wet. It is an ancient teaching in the Catholic tradition that sacraments presuppose faith, and are useless without it. In this book we shall consistently present deacons as sacraments and not just as functionaries, and insist that faith is necessary to see beyond the functionary to the sacrament and what it symbolizes.

Before entering into the body of the work, there are several things we need to clarify for the reader. The first is our use of the term *symbol,* particularly as we apply it to sacrament. Our understanding of symbol is best illustrated quickly by an example. A man and a woman fall in love. The man loves the woman, but the woman does not yet realize it; that is, for her it has not yet been made fully real. For her, the man's love is abstract and remote, and it remains so until he expresses it and embodies it in some action. He writes her a letter; he takes her hand; he kisses her; he tells her, "I love you." In these concrete actions and words, his abstract love is revealed to her, and so also is made real for her. Indeed, not only is his love made real for her, it is also made real for him. In the actions and words, both are confronted by love, are enriched by it, and are provoked to respond to it. The common phrase which is used in our language, namely, *make love,* appears to be very accurate. For in the words and actions, the man's love for the woman, and hers for him, is not only expressed or signified, but is also made concretely real. The effect, love made real for both of them, is due entirely both to the originating love and to the actions and words in which it is realized. The actions and words are called symbols, indeed efficacious symbols, that is, symbols which effect what they symbolize.

The classic ritual actions of the Church, which are normally called sacraments, are symbols. That is, they are actions and words which reveal and make real and celebrate what they symbolize. It is a characteristic note of the Roman Catholic Church that it insists on the sacramentality of the economy of salvation. It perceives three sacramental phases in this economy. The first is *incarnation,* in which the transcendent God is revealed as immanent in the man Jesus; the second is *the Church,* in which the now glorified Jesus is revealed and encountered as real in the gathering of those who believe in him; the third is *sacraments,* in which the Church proclaims and realizes and celebrates its faith in the presence of Jesus and, therefore, of God. The Catholic Church today has no hesitation in speaking of Jesus as the sacrament of God, of the Church as the sacrament of Jesus, and of solemn ritual actions as sacraments of the Church. The writers have no more hesitation in naming the deacon, in the same vein, a sacrament of the Church. That means, as we shall explain, that he makes real in the world, precisely by incarnating them, the Church, Jesus and God.

Though this book is about deacons in the Catholic Church, we do not pretend to know yet all there is to be said about them. Nor do we profess to be writing a book about all the doctrines of the Catholic Church. The Catholic tradition is important to us and we believe that we have been faithful to that tradition in this book, but we have not dealt with everything important in that tradition. Among the realities which we have not treated at length, but for which we wish to profess great respect, is the episcopate. We believe that the role of bishop is one of great sacramental significance in the Church. For it is in the bishop that we find incarnated to the utmost in a diocese that Jesus who is head of the Church. It is the bishop who is to reveal and embody in the diocese in sacramental representation the reality of the Church, of Jesus and of God. We acknowledge that point here, so that our non-treatment of the bishop's important role in the body of the book will not be interpreted as a sign that we believe that his role is insignificant. The bishop, like the deacon and also the priest, is a sacrament of the Church, of Jesus and of God.

We do not deal with him at length in this book, only because we wish to deal with the deacon in as tightly focused a way as possible.

The English word *diaconate* derives from the Greek word *diakonia,* which means service. Since that Greek word is so well known and accepted by deacon people, we shall use *diakonia* throughout this work with no italicized emphasis as if it were an English word. Since every baptized Christian is called to diakonia, to service, every Christian is essentially a deacon. However, this book is about the ordained deacon, the one who is the sacramental embodiment of the call to diakonia that all of us share. We hope that keeping in mind the distinction between all Christians as deacons and ordained deacons will enable the reader to grasp the significant points about the restored diaconate.

Some special acknowledgments are in order. Fourteen years ago we were introduced to the diaconate by Fr. William L. Philbin, a priest of the Archdiocese of Chicago. He was, until his untimely death in 1973, the executive secretary of the Bishops' Committee on the Permanent Diaconate. Our appreciation for Father Philbin was shared by all the early diaconate people because of both his personal holiness and his pastoral insight into the potential of this order. Our love of and dedication to this movement is certainly in part due to the great influence he had in those first years of discovery. The diaconate, as it has evolved in the United States, owes him an enormous debt of gratitude. We are happy to acknowledge that debt here, lest it be forever forgotten.

Because there was no blueprint for the formation of permanent deacons, program directors have been dependent upon each other's advice and assistance from the beginning. Such dependence has been a great grace, for it has created a community of friendship and mutual support. Our relationship with the National Association of Permanent Diaconate Directors has been a very special one. The purpose of the association was to provide a forum for sharing experience from which any and all directors could benefit. It has been that and much more. Many of the conclusions reached in this book surfaced first in discussions with other directors around the United States and Canada. We wish to acknowledge that fact here and to state our gratitude, not only for their insights but also for their friendship.

In Chapter 4, we compare deacon and priest, theologically and "thematically." Selection Research, Incorporated, of Lincoln, Nebraska, is responsible for providing both the instruments and the data that make that comparison possible. We believe that Chapter 4 offers insight into the meanings of both diaconate and priesthood, by clarifying the differences between the deacon and the priest. We hope it is done in such a way that the reader's appreciation of both will be significantly enhanced. The research done by SRI is considered by many to be the most significant contribution to date to the evolving understanding of the diaconate. It has clearly shown who the effective deacon is, and more recent research on the priesthood has done the same for the priest. To support concretely the theoretical information from SRI, we offer deacon stories, especially in Chapter 6. We wish to state here that all those stories are true; names and circumstances have been altered at times to assure confidentiality, but each of the stories is one told by some deacon that we know. They offer yet another way to answer the recurrent question: "What is a deacon?" Both SRI and the stories tell us the same thing: if there is a diaconal identity crisis, it need burden us no more!

We have included as appendices two documents of significance to the permanent diaconate. The one is familiar but not always readily available: *General Norms for Restoring the Permanent Diaconate in the Latin Church,* the motu proprio of Pope Paul VI. The other is not so familiar, and is without title. It was written by the "Original Deacon Circle," a group of German men dedicated to the restoration of the permanent diaconate. It is the document that this group submitted to the fathers of Vatican Council II in 1962. We feel that it is of historical interest to see how those most interested at that time saw the future. We wish to state our thanks to Hanus Kramer, one of that "Circle," who gave the document to us last year in Freiburg, West Germany.

In this introduction of ourselves and of the material of our book, we hope to stimulate other interested parties to share their insights into the experience of deeply touching the lives of others in diaconal ministry. We express serious opinions here, because we believe them and want to share them with you. Our fervent hope is that by such sharing our common experience of incarnation today will expand and deepen.

1.
Questions From Recent History

The history of diaconate in this country has evolved in very interesting ways. People who care about the direction and hopes of diaconate ask questions today that were not asked at the time of its restoration in the United States in the early 1970s. One of the earliest questions was whether *diaconate* was spelled *dia* or *dea* and, humorous as that may sound, that is about where we were in those early days.

A new baby had been created and we did not know what it was going to look like or should look like. Most diocesan directors of diaconate programs came from vocations' offices, which in itself may reveal a great deal about the initial vision of the diaconate. The view was that the deacon was to be found and trained according to the model of priesthood and religious life. Interestingly enough, however, vocations directors did not, in general, stay with the diaconate. The lot fell to others with different vision, a different sense of where this new "vocation material" might go. A few of the directors had the insight that diaconate was a new vocation type, and that it could evolve into an entirely new ministry.

Early meetings of diaconate directors looked at the motu proprio of Pope Paul VI, *Sacrum Ordinem Diaconatus*, issued in 1967, which restored the diaconate as a permanent state in the Catholic Church. The document focused primarily upon those nations usually referred to as the "third world," where foreign missionaries served the native church. The fathers of Vatican II had envisioned a role of indigenous leadership for deacons in those nations, a role that was to be primarily liturgical and administrative. Such a role was something of a turnabout from the one envisioned by the "Original Deacon Circle," a group of men in and around Munich, West Germany. This circle grew out of a group of men who were interned at Dachau prison camp during World War II. While in prison, they wondered about how the

11

Church could be resurrected from the ravages of the war. After their release, the group continued to meet and to create hope for the diaconate as something that would contribute to the needed resurrection. They involved themselves in Catholic Action, and were deeply concerned to find a hopeful image that the Church could offer to the German people in particular. Over a period of years, members of this "Deacon Circle" continued to evolve in their purposes and in their sense of the diaconate. During the Second Vatican Council the group sent a request to the assembled bishops, asking them formally to re-establish the diaconate as a permanent state in the Catholic Church. That document, which appears as an appendix to this book, presents a vision of diaconate which sees the deacon as performing service-tasks as needed in the Church.

That document, prepared with the assistance of theologians Karl Rahner and Yves Congar, did not alone recreate the diaconate. But the vision and the request it put forward found such favor with the fathers of the Council that they mandated twice, in their Constitution on the Church (n. 29) and in their Declaration on the Missions (n. 16), that the diaconate be restored to the orders of the Church as a permanent state. That mandate, we must realize, had limited impact. For the Council of Trent in the sixteenth century had also mandated the restoration of the diaconate, and nothing had happened. Until Pope Paul VI published his motu proprio, Vatican II's mandate could have gone the way of Trent's. After the publication of the motu proprio, the bishops of the United States decided to restore the diaconate in this country. They were concerned for the American third world—blacks, Mexican-Americans, Cubans and other minority groups—because that focus was in the Vatican II documents and in the motu proprio. However, from the earliest days, directors of diaconate programs have customarily been Caucasian men. And, both then and now, they have asked themselves: "How can we establish the diaconate among minorities?" The question persists, for the diaconate in this country remains an overwhelmingly white middle class institution.

The first guidelines for the restoration of the diaconate in the United States were approved by the Bishops' Committee on the Diaconate in 1969. Fr. William Philbin from Chicago was appointed executive secretary of that committee and given the task of providing guidance for dioceses to get programs started on the local level. Philbin had talents for enabling directors to look at what was developing, for bringing varied questions together and for providing a platform on which those questions could be discussed. He was not an answer man, but a skilled asker of questions that needed to be asked. The most significant and most recurring question has been: "What, precisely, is a permanent deacon?" With the passage of time and the ordination of many outstanding deacons, we are now in a position to answer that question.

It is not our purpose to restate the history of the diaconate. Readers are encouraged to consult James Barnett's study entitled *The Diaconate: A Full and Equal Order,* which contains a thorough and clear study of the history and development of the diaconate in earlier times. The question that arises today is whether there is continuity between the diaconate that died in the ninth century and the permanent diaconate of the twentieth century. In his address to the directors of permanent diaconate programs in the United States at their convention in 1983, historical theologian Michael Himes stressed rather the discontinuity. He insisted that we are dealing with a brand new diaconate institution, and he added that the ancient diaconate ought to be considered as only secondary. We are, he argued, creating a new order, and we should do that with enthusiasm and with creativity instead of checking backward to see if we are in line with the past. Instead of questions like: "Did deacons preach in the early Church?" we should ask: "Do we want deacons to preach in today's Church?"

Another recurring question has been: "Why was the permanent diaconate eclipsed in the first millennium?" The answer is, in large part, that the rise of sacerdotalism in the ninth century destroyed the diaconate as an independent order. Sacerdotalism is an overemphasis on the power invested in the priesthood. History suggests that a power-struggle between deacons and priests at that time left the priesthood with all the power, absorbing into itself the role of deacon, which is why even today everyone who is ordained a priest must be ordained a deacon first. An obvious question today is this: Does every priest need to approach priesthood through diaconate? There is a groundswell among diaconate people answering that question negatively, and suggesting that the transitional diaconate be done away with. That would remove the anomaly of trying to restore the diaconate as a permanent order while still retaining it as a transitional order. The study of life themes in priests and deacons shows that there are essential differences between the two. The most important difference is that the priest is predominantly a leader and the deacon is predominantly a helper.

Another frequently asked question is: "Why ordain deacons at all? Isn't everyone called to diakonia?" The question, which alludes to every Christian's call to a life of diakonia, has been a helpful one, for it has forced us to look at the meaning of baptism and ordination and at the relationship between them. The question can be rephrased in this way: "If every Christian is called by baptism to a life of diakonia, why would we want to go further and ordain some of them to the diaconate?"

A new element has evolved in the diaconate, namely, an intense, intimate community experience and what it offers to ministerial people who do not lead a common life. That experience raises the question of the value to someone called to ministry in today's Church of belonging to a community which mediates an ongoing and lived experience of Jesus. The question is of great concern in a Church in which long-established ministerial roles are not relinquished easily. But, even in a Church in which ministers shared easily their ministerial roles and functions, the question would remain. Do ministers need an ongoing community experience to sustain them and to call them constantly to an accountable ministerial relationship with the people to whom they minister?

Directors of diaconate formation programs in the early days, with rare exceptions, were priests. For the most part, these dedicated men were trying to design programs which would educate and form deacon candidates following a model commonly referred to as "the seminary model." In that model, the teacher stands in front of the class, lectures to them, gives them papers to write and tests to pass, and grades them at the end of the term. He also provides retreat experiences. Candidates for the diaconate, who fell mostly in the range from 35–50 years old, had not been to school for many years. They were enthusiastic about learning, but in general they had no firm study habits. For the most part the seminary approach, which educated the mind but not the person, did not have a great effect on their lives. In the early days some interested wives would sit in on the classes with their husbands. Eventually, however, a few women got into leadership roles or at least supportive roles in the programs and we began to see the role of the wife differently.

Some program directors began to feel that the call of the wife to the diaconate was at least as strong as it was for the husband. There are many ramifications of this situation, and we have to look at them, since the vast majority of men training for the diaconate are joined to women by God with the injunction: "What God has joined together let not man put asunder" (Mt 19:6). That raises another question, related to husband and wife togetherness, concerning the relationship of marriage and orders. Few appear willing to confront that question positively and with confidence. We shall try to do so later.

There are still other issues concerning women and the diaconate. Early in the history of the restoration in the United States, discussion surfaced about the ordination of women to the diaconate. In general, directors have always been supportive of the call of women to ordination. It should be noted that when Pope Paul VI issued his "Declaration on the Question of the Admission of Women to the Ministerial Priesthood" in 1977, denying the possibility of the ordination of women to the priesthood, he made no mention whatever of the possibility of ordaining women to the diaconate. The argument of that Declaration was described by Karl Rahner as "none too lucid." But lucid or not, it has no bearing whatever, nor was it intended to have any bearing, on the question of the admission of women to the ordained diaconate.

Another of the significant issues that has arisen over the years is the mutual relationship of diaconate and priesthood. The issue has two focuses, one theological, the other emotional. The first is the theological connection and distinction of priest and deacon; the second is the emotional connection and distinction between them. At least some of the emotion revolves around "power." Many priests were trained in and still operate out of an institutional model of the Church. Once appointed pastors of parishes, they have philosophical and emotional problems with sharing ministry. The problems exist not only between priests and deacons, but also between priests and parish councils, between priests and talented lay people. The problems derive theologically from the institutional model of the Church, which presents both bishops and priests as ministers of power, and all other ministers (if they can be called ministers at all) as subordinate to them. That way of describing the Church does not permit an imaging of the diaconate as an order in its own right, connected to but not lesser than the priesthood. A personal investment in such a model of ministerial hierarchy cannot but create emotional difficulties when questions of shared ministry and shared power arise.

There are many priests who operate out of a vision of Church in which they are gifted with power and in which the deacon appears as threatening some of that power. Laity also frequently work out of that same vision of Church, and they ask what kind of power a deacon has. The deacon himself can be trapped into asking, and trying to answer, the same kind of question. It is not surprising, then, that priests, deacons and laity frequently ask a predictable American question: "But what do deacons *do*?" That question usually means "What power do deacons have that priests and laity do not have?"

Very early in the modern history of the diaconate we heard it said that the ordination of permanent deacons should help to clarify roles in the Church. It should clarify for the lay person what it means to be a lay person and for the priest what it means to be a priest. We would like to consider some facets of that expectation. Frequently we hear criticisms of the diaconate as an institution which does not have many leaders. But are deacons leaders? Are they supposed to be leaders? And if they are leaders, in what kind of relationship do they stand vis-à-vis priests, whom we believe to be called clearly to serve as spiritual leaders at the parish level?

A horde of questions arise after ordination to the diaconate. "*Where* is he a deacon? *How* is he a deacon? *When* is he a deacon? *Why* is he a deacon? *With whom* is he a deacon? *Who* chooses him to be a deacon in the first place?" There are even questions the deacon tends to ask himself: "Why is the Church ordaining deacons? What is my significance in the Church in the 1980s?" And then there are the questions asked of wives of men who are to be ordained. "Aren't you proud of him? Isn't it wonderful that your husband is going to be ordained a deacon?" The response of women who have journeyed with their husbands all the way through the preparatory program is often one of great frustration—and of bewilderment. They wonder, and we wonder with them, if the real question being asked is: "Aren't you proud of him now that he is being promoted into the clerical state where he will have power?" "What kind of magic can he perform now?" might also phrase it well. No question is asked about the wife's talent or about her call to diakonia.

One final question that we have been asked consistently over the years is this: "What type of men apply for ordination to the permanent diaconate?" Our experience indicates that the answer is that there has been a significant evolution in the type. In the late 1960s and the early 1970s, most people had a passive relationship to the Church which was quite different from the active one they have today. Shared responsibility was almost an unknown reality. Lay apostolate was in practice still the participation of the laity in the work of the hierarchy. The Second Vatican Council caused a major shift in that thinking. Though the practice still lags seriously behind the theology and though limitations still are imposed upon lay persons seeking ministerial roles in the Church, reflecting an attitude that is still seriously doubtful about the call of laity to ministry, that theological shift has occurred. Most men applying now for admission to diaconal ordination conceive their ministerial role in a much more active sense than did candidates in the early days. Today, men seeking ordination to the diaconate come from a range of developmental stages and with a range of attitudes toward ministry that are vastly different from those who sought entrance in the early days. Also, the evolving place of women in the overall society is being reflected among women in the Church who are seeking to be ordained to the diaconate. At least some are demanding full participation in training programs with their husbands.

In this chapter we have sought only to articulate questions that have evolved out of the lived experience of the diaconate over the past fifteen years. We wanted to see for ourselves, and to allow you to see, how those questions have risen out of history that is both ancient and very new in our Church. We have not created the questions, but rather we have encountered them as the diaconate has developed in our midst and with our participation. We believe that the ultimate answers to those questions still lie in the future that our Church has the task and the privilege of helping to create. We believe that as we find those answers and create that future for the diaconate we shall find also that the future is in glorious continuity with the past.

2.

The Human Jesus:
Sacrament of God

*I*n the first chapter, we raised some questions that have evolved in the history of the diaconate. A problem with raising questions so relentlessly is that we may become impatient for quick answers. But we believe that we have not yet raised the root question about ministry in the Church, namely, the relationship of that ministry to Jesus who is the root of everything that is Christian. We need to find out if Jesus was a deacon. And if he was a deacon, how was he a deacon, and what did he do as a deacon? We begin this chapter, therefore, by asking "Who is Jesus?" and "What was he all about?" and "What does he have to say to us today about ministry in general, and about diaconal ministry in particular?"

The Gospels report that Jesus asked his disciples: "Who do men say that I am?" (Mk 8:27). The responses are varied and very interesting, but Matthew tells us that the one that Jesus affirmed was Peter's reply, "You are the Christ, the Son of the living God" (16:16). Catholic theology has consistently taught that Jesus was the Son of God in the flesh, that he was the incarnation of God in a human form. We would like to consider that incarnation from the perspective of the humanity of Jesus. What is incarnation really about, especially in view of St. Paul's saying that Jesus emptied himself of divinity, took on the form of a slave, and became obedient even unto death? (Phil 2:5–8).

We Christians believe that Jesus was not only the incarnation of the divine, but also the incarnation of the human. That certainly is in accord with the catechism most of us learned when we were young, which taught that he was perfect God and perfect man. But the perfect God, Catholic theology teaches, is revealed specifically in the perfect man, and to gain insight into his divinity, we must have insight first into his humanity. If we can discern how God is revealed in the man from Nazareth, then we might be able to discern also how Jesus himself is revealed in

23

that community of men and women we call his Church and his body. By discerning the man in Jesus, we might discover also the deacon in him, and the nature of the ministering Christian. Paradoxically, to discover the divinity of Jesus we need to balance the traditional overemphasis on that divinity with a renewed emphasis on his humanity, just as he needed to empty himself of divinity in order to reveal it in and through his humanity. It is by focusing on the humanity of Jesus, we believe, that we will discover the deeper answer to his question: "Who do you say that I am?" We do not deny his divinity, but seek only to expose his humanity to the fullest.

The Gospels present Jesus to us as a very free person. At age twelve, they suggest, he already seems to know and accept himself. He seems to realize that he has a very special relationship to God as his Father. He seems to have his priorities straight, and the Father's will is first, even before the concern of his parents. His freedom, it seems, is the operational agreement between his feelings and his actions. Nothing outside himself, except the Father's will, controls his behavior. In addition to that form of assertive freedom, Jesus appears to have in his nature to the highest degree the capacity of relating. He must have been a most approachable man, for the rejects of his society approached him, even against the law! His charisma for preaching must have been astounding to hold great numbers of people for long hours. His capacity to empathize with the hurting, to touch deeply the lives of people, is revealed in most of the Gospel stories of healing. He is pictured for us as a warm, loving human being whose concern for the downtrodden calls him regularly to go beyond the laws of his society.

Using our imaginations, we would like to recreate some of the stories in the Gospels to stimulate our thinking about Jesus the minister, especially as we see therein his humanity. To do so, we would like to turn first to the familiar story of Zacchaeus, the tax collector, money changer, thief (Lk 19:1–10).

In our minds' eye we see the disciples of Jesus in Jericho a few days prior to his coming to preach about the kingdom. They discover among other things that this Zacchaeus was the town reject. To a good Jew of his day his past was sordid. He had been born illegitimate, was something of a midget, had never been invited to play with other children when he was young. He was, in the words of modern psychologists, a not okay person. But Zacchaeus had found a great way to get even. He took a job working with the Romans. So what if he was called unclean for working with them; it was nothing new to him. During his whole life he had been told he was unclean. He derived a special pleasure now from cheating Jews and becoming wealthy at their expense. But he was still the least affirmed man in Jericho.

Jesus comes to Jericho. He singles Zacchaeus out of the crowd. Zacchaeus is in a sycamore tree, and for good reason. He had been changing money for the large crowd gathered in town because Jesus was coming. As a result he is late, and since he is short of stature, he climbs the tree to be able to see. Now the sycamore tree has always been, and still remains, an enemy of the desert people. It sucks up the little water there is, but produces nothing. The Gospel story is so picturesque and apt, since the sycamore tree almost perfectly describes Zacchaeus, sucking up the money of the people, but producing nothing! And yet this is the man Jesus affirms in front of the whole crowd. It may be that is the first serious affirmation the man ever receives, and it comes from Jesus.

To see the freedom of Jesus operate before the eyes of the crowd is overwhelming. He offers to this little man the simple gesture of acceptance, not for what he does in life, but merely because he is a man. A feeling comes to us that Jesus needed to get Zacchaeus "out of the tree," and to have him invite Jesus into his "house," that is, into his life. Something wonderful happens: it is called being set free! In the interaction described in the Gospel, Jesus says: "I want to spend the day with you." Might that be translated: "I want to share my life with you"? Such a human offer of acceptance, affirmation, and hope creates in Zacchaeus a conversion response which all who have received acceptance will recognize, and he is moved to announce that he will return whatever he has stolen and will give half of his possessions to the poor. In his turn, Jesus is moved to announce that "today salvation has come to your house." Salvation is spelled J-E-S-U-S. Jesus had been allowed into Zacchaeus' life, and the wealthy sycamore tree was no more! He had been set free, from rejection, self-hatred and emptiness.

The Zacchaeus story is an action form of the parable of the sower going out to sow. In his interaction with Zacchaeus, Jesus shows us how the parable works. The ground that is Zacchaeus has been stomped on for a lifetime. Manure had been dumped on him by the truckload, until he was literally burned up. Jesus takes that soil, cultivates it, warms it, waters it, plants the seed in Zacchaeus, and the seed is able to grow. Before Jesus can do that, he has to get into Zacchaeus' house. He cannot do it while Zacchaeus is still up the sycamore tree. He has to get him out of the tree and into his house. The human interchange happens. Jesus plants himself in the life of Zacchaeus and sets him free.

Jesus shows his ministerial style in the parable of the sower. He is the seed who wants to be planted in the various types of people available. Some, like Zacchaeus, have been stomped down, made hard, infertile, closed, and dry. If they remain that way, no planting will ever penetrate the surface. The rocky ground depicts the superficially open who, deeper down, are hard, impenetrable, non-accepting, and basically closed to anyone ever entering their lives with any depth. There is initial, superficial response, but no continuing conversion of life. The "thorns" among whom Jesus is sown are those on the wayside, outside the mainstream of life. The cares of the world are wrapped up in drugs, sex, power, money, and the planted word is easily choked. Then there is the good ground, where the seed can produce great response and fruit up to one hundredfold. Jesus appears to minister in a way that invites the various types of soil to react to him. Zacchaeus is shown as the hard ground, but Jesus cultivates the soil with love, acceptance, affirmation, and hope. Such great human qualities are capable of setting a person free. Other stories, such as that of the woman caught in adultery, call out of Jesus the same type of human understanding and loving acceptance. His non-judgmental character allows him to accept people as who they are. That is cultivating the soil, watering it, fertilizing it, warming it, and calling it to produce new life. He seems to say that his ministry is planting *himself* in the lives of people. They appear as different forms of soil, but his job is to love them and thereby to cultivate and prepare the soil for planting.

Further evidence of how Jesus attempts to plant himself appears in the story of the rich young man (Mt 19:16–22). He runs up to Jesus and asks for a quick fix on entering the kingdom. Jesus calmly reacts, suggesting the normal Jewish way of keeping the law. The young man's response tells Jesus that he is imprisoned by the gold bars of his riches. Jesus assures him that freedom from his prison involves giving up his wealth, and he invites him to do just that. The young man goes away very sad, because he has many possessions. The sower is outside the prison, throwing seed at the cell, but the cell is made of gold, as hard a metal as there is.

In this story we see Jesus not only as free in himself, but also as offering freedom to others and as respecting even the freedom to say no. He does not say to the young man: "Now, let's look at all your options, and see if we can work out some form of deal!" He lets him go. He offers him freedom, even the freedom to go away sad. Jesus knows he is the turning point in the life of every man, woman, and child, and yet he lets the rich young man walk away. He invites the young man to come into his life, to sell what he has, to give it to the poor, and to follow Jesus, but he leaves him free to accept or reject the invitation. Such an invitation to freedom is at the heart of what Jesus' ministry is about. He offers the freedom of a love relationship that calls those he touches to know they are loved, that they are significant, that they are worthwhile. It is a love relationship that asks those he touches to put away guilt and fear, anxiety and prejudice, ignorance and blindness, despair, infidelity and paralysis. It is a love relationship that calls people to healing, to reconciliation, to hope, to meaning. It is a love relationship that invites people to see through Jesus' human qualities to God immanent in his humanity. He says in so many words and actions: "See through my humanity and you will catch a glimpse of God who loves you no matter what!"

Looking further at the humanity of Jesus reflected in the Gospels, we find the multiplication of loaves and fishes revealing more about the ministerial style of Jesus (Mt 14:13–21). The large crowd had been listening to Jesus all day long, and the disciples are forced to remind him not only that it is late in the day, but also that the people are hungry. Jesus responds: "Give them something to eat." They declare, facetiously, that there is no way such a crowd can eat, for all that is available is a couple of loaves of bread and a few fish belonging to a youngster in the crowd. Even if they could use the food, what would that be among such a large group? The response of Jesus gets right to the heart of the matter. He tells them, in effect, "Don't talk to me about what you do *not* have; do something with what you *do* have." Then he gives the formula for feeding crowds: claim what you do have, look to heaven to place God in what you are about to offer, and then give it away freely. The end result is that not only are people fed, but also the leftovers fill a perfect number of baskets. Even the youngster has enough to take home with him.

The next day, we are told, the crowd returns to watch the "magician" at work and to get a free meal. Jesus, however, has something else in mind, namely, talk about a different bread and a different drink. He offers them himself. He tells them that if they want to live life to the fullest, in fact if they want to live at all, they are to share his humanity, filled with God. "Unless you eat me as the ordinary stuff of life, and drink my blood (blood is life), unless you find LIFE himself in the ordinary stuff of life, you will never discover the meaning of incarnation. You will never see how God has enfleshed himself in the ordinary. Unless you eat the flesh of the Son of Man and drink his blood, you will not have life in you. When you learn to eat the flesh and drink the blood of my humanity, you will never die. You will have life everlasting."

The crowd misses his point. They are certain he is asking them to become cannibals, and their response is to leave. The disciples have the same questions about his meaning. Jesus turns to them and asks them if they will leave too. "Where would we go? You have the words of eternal life." He doesn't call the crowd back, saying: "Hey, come back, I am speaking symbolically. I will ask you to eat blessed bread and wine, that's all. Please, I think you have misunderstood my meaning. Come back. After all, I have come to save you!" He says only: "He who eats my flesh and drinks my blood has life everlasting." Jesus again allows people to be free—free to reject him, his message, his salvation. In effect he is allowing them to reject the great secret of life, that you become what you consume. What you do with life, what you consume of life—that becomes your life.

The Gospels portray Jesus also as showing courage in the face of the enemies who seek to destroy him. He never shrinks from them. He shows his courage before Annas, Caiaphas, and Pilate, and before the Pharisees and the powerful, whom he confronts about heaping burdens on the backs of the poor and then doing nothing to lighten them. In the claiming of his identity, "Before Abraham was, I am" (Jn 8:58), he shows the courage to risk the accusation of blasphemy. That accusation led to his ultimate act of courage, namely, his giving up of himself to death on a tree.

Our reading of the Gospel clarifies for us that Jesus' humanity is very authentic. To be authentic a person needs to be free, and needs to be able to let others be free. He needs to be open about who he is and what he has to offer. The authenticity of Jesus allows him to be fully receptive of people who present themselves to him, not for what they have done, right or wrong, but for what they are. To be so open to people is humanity reaching to its limit, incarnating all that is meant by human and suggesting what it must mean to be divine.

Being authentic, Jesus is not afraid to call people to be a lot more than they have been, nor is he afraid to call them to accountability about the negative ways in which they relate with others, as he does constantly with the Pharisees. Authentic people are those who have the courage to claim every gift they have and to realize that it is in giving themselves away that they come to know who they are. That might be the definition of the great lover: one who gives himself or herself away in order to find himself or herself. It is certainly what Jesus, the great lover, did. He gave himself away to others, to other men and women to be sure, but above all to the other who was his Father. Indeed, his giving of himself to that Father, his obedience to that Father's will, as we customarily say, is the key to understanding the meaning of his life. That obedience is to be understood in the sense that Jesus knew deeply in his human heart that everything that he was about needed to be in accord with what God called him to do in life. And what he felt called to do, we believe, was to plant himself in the lives of people and to set them free to see God. His life was to be in the trenches with the tax collector, the prostitute, the sick, the possessed, all the lepers of society. God called him to use everything he had within his humanity to plant himself in their lives and thereby set them free. To confess that Jesus is the incarnation of humanity is to confess that he is the model of and for humanity, that he is what we are called to be, both as humans and as ministers, or, better, as human ministers. We are called, therefore, to plant ourselves in the lives of people and to set them free to see God as Jesus did.

The New Testament portrays very clearly that in his human life Jesus was seen to be special, so special that slowly people came to see and to say that God was with him. Eventually, and also slowly, they came to see and to say not only that God was with him, but also that he himself was God in human form. There is a mystery which envelops human life, a mystery which religious men and women name God. The peak-human life of Jesus of Nazareth suggested to some men and women in the first century that in him the mystery had been definitively unveiled. They confessed that this man, who lived humanity to its very limit, revealed at that limit not only what it was like to be man, but also what it was like to be God. The man who was free incarnated a God who is freedom. The man who was loving incarnated a God who is love. The man who was gracious incarnated a God who is grace. The man who proclaimed his life-work as a work of service for others (Mk 10:45) incarnated a God who is supremely for others. We believe that it can be said that, above all, Jesus served the presence of God within humanity by incarnating it in himself and by allowing others to see it in him. We have no hesitation, therefore, in naming him the deacon of the presence of God.

And what of us who want to be the disciples of Jesus and the ministers of his Gospel? God calls us, in and through this Jesus, to be like him, to be the perfect men and women we can be. He calls us to be such men and women by planting ourselves in the lives of others so that he can work and reveal himself in them. That is a task we can manage, at least with his help. We can study Jesus and try to become like him as we minister with people. That perfect man is, in his humanity, also the perfect minister, indeed the perfect deacon. That immediately raises an important question. What kind of people are capable of being so fully human that, like Jesus, they can plant themselves in the lives of others and enable them to see God? In short, what kind of human qualities should we look for in ministers? We shall answer those questions in Chapter 4.

3.

The Human Church:
Sacrament of Jesus

Several years ago, two deacons were working together in a section at a factory in the city. They were new to the particular section, and noticed that the group of twenty-two men and women was a very negative one. The verbal interaction was destructive and lacking in affirmation. The air was blue with foul language and sexual innuendos, and the reading material was the latest pornographic epic. The deacons noticed that the end of the work day came as a great relief; they noticed too that the negativity at work spilled over into negativity at home. They decided to do something about it. They divided the group and within a couple of weeks they had visited one on one with each member. They spent time with individuals, got to know them, listened to their stories, and affirmed them. They soon noticed that the language began to change, and the pornography disappeared. They noticed also that the group became more positive toward each other, with real friendships forming. One day, one of the others suggested that all gather for breakfast on Saturday, their day off, and spend some time discussing the Bible and praying together. They asked the deacons, of course, to lead them. Before long everyone remarked how the end of the day was a joyful occurrence, as the men and women looked forward to going home to their spouses and children. The two deacons mentioned to each other what a pleasure it was now to go to work.

The beauty of that parable is that it is a true story. It is what deacons do in general to make the humanity of Jesus real for the people around them. Prior to the intervention of the two deacons, the above group created lepers every day, and the spirit at work reflected that disease, making a miserable day for everyone. Bringing that spirit home to spouse and children had leprous effects on family life. But when the workers started to affirm one another they came alive as a group, bringing new life both to their work and to their family relationships. The simple human

interaction of love set them all free. Now that is what incarnation is about today. And that is what this chapter is about. The
previous chapter was about Jesus and how God was seen to be
incarnated in him. The present chapter is about how Jesus has
left himself incarnate in the world, and how he, the incarnation
of God, becomes incarnate in us, the Church. It is about how
the Church's ministers, like the two deacons in the factory, set
people free by planting themselves in their lives and by incarnating there the presence of Jesus and of God.

But before entering into that discussion, we must clarify
something first. The English word *Church* is a word that is very
commonly used. It is also a word that has a range of meanings,
which makes it a word that can be the source of as much mis-
communication as of communication. Before proceeding, therefore, to consider the nature of the Church in this chapter, we
must clarify the meaning of the word as we shall use it.

The early Christians used the Greek word *ekklesia* to describe themselves. This word means "the gathering of people
called together by a herald." It is in this sense that *ekklesia* is
used in the New Testament, and it is in this same sense that we
shall use the English word *Church* throughout this book. We believe that the herald who calls the Church together is God, and
it is in response to his call that we gather. What God calls the
Church to be is what Paul names the body of Christ. He speaks
passionately of its incarnational function. "As many of you as
were baptized into Christ have put on Christ. There is neither
Jew nor Greek, there is neither slave nor free, there is neither
male nor female; for you are all one person in Christ Jesus" (Gal
3:27–28). The Church is Christ in very human form.

The ritual of baptism proclaims, makes real and celebrates
a person's initiation into the Christian Church. As God trans-
formed Jesus from death to life and anointed him as the Christ,
so also he transforms those who are baptized from ritual death
to ritual newness of life and anoints them as other Christs.

When the early Christians interpreted what had happened to them in baptism as a "new creation" (2 Cor 5:17; Gal 6:15), or as being "born of water and the Spirit" (Jn 3:5), they were talking about a transformation in the depths of their being. And there was the rub. For all its wonder, the new creation and the new birth effected only a beginning. For becoming a Christian demands more than ritual baptism; it demands also a life lived in imitation of Jesus, the original Christ. Cyprian of Carthage, an early Father of the Church, always concerned with baptismal and Christian life, is quite clear about this: putting on Christ in baptism is meaningless if the baptized does not follow the life of Christ. "If we have put Christ on," he argues, "we ought to go forward according to the example of Christ." That advice returns us to the Church, the gathering of the faithful.

The Church is the elect of God and the body of Christ. It is composed of those men and women whom God has called to believe in his presence in Jesus, and who have responded to that call by believing and by bonding themselves in baptism to live in community with Christ and with one another. The Church is essentially community. But it is more than just community. It is community that is also, by its relationship with Christ, "a kind of sacrament," as Vatican II put it. In the terminology of medieval Scholasticism, that means that the Church is, on the one hand, a community of human believers and, on the other hand, both a sign and an instrument of grace. In the terminology of modern sacramental theology, it means that the human community called the Church is also a symbol of grace in the world, that is, it reveals and makes real and celebrates the presence of Christ and his God. In the words of the classical Catholic theology in which Jesus incarnates the invisible God, the believing Church incarnates a now just as invisible Jesus. It is precisely because the Church incarnates in the world Jesus, who is the Christ, that it is called the body of Christ.

The Church, then, is a double-tiered reality. On the one

hand, it is the gathering of the believers Tom, Dick, and Sharon; and, on the other hand, in that gathering is symboled the presence of Jesus and the gracious God he serves. To "see" the presence of Jesus and of God in the gathered presence of Tom and Dick and Sharon, of course, takes as much faith as it takes to "see" the presence of God in the man Jesus. But the Church is essentially a community of faith; it is nothing without faith. The Church is not for itself; its ministry is not for itself. The Church and ministry are to incarnate Jesus in human history, and so to incarnate also God. If Jesus was and is the minister, the servant, the deacon (cf. Mk 10:45) of the presence of God, the Church which is his body will, of necessity, be the minister, the servant, the deacon of that very same personal presence. The Church, as has been so often said because it so often needed to be said, is not the kingdom of God, but the minister of the kingdom; it is not the absolute presence of God, but the servant of that presence; it is not the grace of God, but the deacon of that grace. It ministers and serves and deacons (at least in Greek that is a verb!) by incarnating in the world, by being in the world, the body of Jesus who is the anointed deacon of the presence of God. Inherent in the call to be the Church is the call to be deacon of the presence of God.

In the New Testament, indeed in the whole pre-Nicene era, ministry is a function of the Church. There are individual ministers, a great variety of them, ranging from the triad of apostle, prophet, teacher, which we find in the genuinely Pauline letters (cf. 1 Cor 12:4–12, 28; Rom 12:4–8; Eph 4:11–14), to that other triad of bishop, presbyter, deacon, which we find at the opening of the second century. But all of those ministers are ministers of the Church; they are ministers whom the Church recognizes as its own because it recognizes them as servants and deacons doing the very service which it itself is called to do.

Luke opens his account of Jesus' ministry with a pregnant quotation from Isaiah: "The Spirit of the Lord is upon me, because he has anointed me to preach good news to the poor. He has sent me to proclaim release to the captives, and recovering of sight to the blind, to set at liberty those who are oppressed" (4:18–19; see 4:43). Jesus, it is clear, has a strong sense of being anointed and sent, not only to preach in words the presence of the kingdom, but also to confront in actions whatever might obscure that presence. He feels sent, however, as Mark points out, not to be served but to serve, and he instructs his disciples with no equivocation that the way to be the first in the kingdom of God is to do just that. He invites them to be the servant of all (Mk 9:35). He leaves no doubt as to how he sees his ministry; it is diakonia. It cannot be otherwise in the Church which incarnates him in the world. There is ministry in the Church, but it is diakonia of the presence of God; there are ministers in the Church, but they are deacons of the presence of God; there is power in the Church, but it is power that is exercised in service, not in domination. The Church, just like Jesus, is the deacon of the presence of God in the world. Like him too, it exercises its diakonia by incarnating, that is, by making explicitly present in words and in deeds in the world, the Christ and the God who sent him and anointed him to be his deacon.

To make the Church an effective symbol each member has to live up to the call and the demand to be symbol of Christ and of God in the world. Each and every one is called, that is, to minister as the Church is called to minister. Each is called, that is, to diakonia. Each and every one who responds to that call in diakonia is by that very fact a deacon in the Church. That, of course, is not to say that each and every one is ordained into the order of deacon. It is to say something much more important than that, and much more radical. It is to say that each and every member of the Church who answers the call to be of service is by that very fact a minister of the Church, a servant of the Church, a deacon of the Church.

A question we have been asked persistently is this: "What

is a deacon?" An answer we have persistently given is this: "A deacon is a member of the Church who, in response to God's perceived election and call, reaches out to be of service in the Church and, in this way, incarnates the presence of Jesus, who is the deacon of the presence of God." Jesus not only preached in words the presence of God but also acted to confront situations in which that presence might be obscured. So must it be with the Church's deacon. As Jesus goes to the house of Simon the leper and allows a woman, whom the law has branded, to touch him and anoint him (Mk 14:3–9), so the deacon of his presence will go to the branded and the dispossessed of his society. As Jesus heals the mother of Peter's wife (Mk 1:29–31), so the deacon in his Church will seek to heal and console and reconcile wherever he sees that healing and consoling and reconciling are needed. In his words he proclaims in our troubled world the presence of Christ and of God; in his deeds he symbolizes in an often uncaring world that same gracious God. Where such a deacon is, there is the deacon-Church, there is the deacon-Christ, there is grace, there is God. Where such a deacon is, there Church, Christ and God are truly celebrated and made real.

The foregoing is an initial answer to the common question: "What is a deacon?" Every time we have answered the question as above, namely, a deacon is one who reaches out to be of service in the Church, the response has always been, "I have been doing that for years, so what difference will ordination make?" Ordination, we believe, does make a difference. But before we ask about the difference between an unordained deacon and an ordained deacon, we prefer to ask what is the same about them. For finding out what is the same about them will throw a great deal of light on what is different about them.

We have long known an outstanding deacon. For years he gave hours and hours of his time to the service of disillusioned and disturbed young people. Eventually he sought to become an ordained deacon, and on the day he was ordained he asked him-

self, and us: "What deacon stuff do I do now?" It had not occurred to him that he had been doing "deacon stuff" all those
years, and if he needed "ordained deacon stuff" all he needed to
do was to continue doing what he had been doing. When we told
him that, however, he balked. "Ordination must make a difference," he thought, and therefore there must be special deacon
stuff that one does after it. Now we shall state here, and return
to it again and again throughout this book, that training and ordination never made a deacon out of a non-deacon. All the outstanding ordained deacons that we know or have heard of were
outstanding deacons long before they entered the training program and long before they were ordained to the order of deacon.
All the ineffective deacons that we know, and it is pointless to
pretend that there are none such, are ineffective largely because
they were not effective deacons prior to ordination and looked for
ordination to make a difference, to give them some power that
would make them deacons. When it did not, they asked themselves and us: "What good is ordination since it makes no difference?"

But ordination does make a difference. The difference,
however, is not that it takes someone who is not a deacon and
transforms him into one. The difference is not that ordination
gives a person a power that he did not have before and that now
enables him to do "deacon stuff." To see what difference ordination makes to a person it is crucial to see first what difference
it does not make—that is, to see what is the same about the person after ordination. And what is the same is quite evident. The
charism of diakonia that he had prior to ordination remains the
same; the service he did on behalf of the Church remains
the same; the ministry he did remains the same. If diakonia is
the same both before and after ordination, what difference does
ordination make? The difference may lie more in the Church
than in the ordained person.

What it comes down to is this. The Church recognizes in

the person seeking ordination to the diaconate a demonstrated talent and charism for diakonia. It recognizes in him one whose diakonia is the very ministry the Church is called and sent to perform. It recognizes in him one who symbolizes in the world the presence of Jesus and, therefore, also the presence of grace and of God. It recognizes him, in short, as an incarnation of Church. In ordination it *publicizes* this recognition, that is, it proclaims in public that this person being ordained is the kind of person it itself is called and sent to be, and it designates him now to be its officially sanctioned representative symbol of diakonia. After ordination to the diaconate there is, indeed, a difference. There is, first of all, a difference in the Church. By ordaining this person it has acknowledged something that it had never acknowledged before, namely, that this man is a deacon and, in his diaconate, an outstanding symbol of the Church itself, and therefore of the Christ whose sacrament it is, and therefore of God whose sacrament Christ is. Its ordination of him affirms in him the talent-charism for the diaconate, and affirms in itself the ongoing commitment to be a deacon-Church. This affirmation ordains this deacon to be an exemplar of diakonia to the whole Church.

There is also a difference in the ordained deacon. Prior to ordination he already was a deacon, for already he had answered the call to diakonia on behalf of the Church and of Christ whose body it is. Now he receives an affirmation from the Church that the ministry he does is the Church's ministry, and he receives an ordination to continue to do that ministry, now not only as a private member, but also as a publicly and solemnly designated representative, of the Church. As an ordained deacon he performs not only the diakonia he always performed, but also a new and solemn one. Now he symbols for the Church and all its members what it and they are, and calls them to be what he and they are, namely, deacons in the Church of the presence of Christ, of grace, of God. He does that symboling by being the deacon he was long prior to ordination and by doing the diakonia he always did. An ordained deacon, therefore, is ordained into a very special diakonia, a ministry of calling and enabling others in the Church to be deacons too. That ministry is to be understood essentially as *service,* not as *power.* Or perhaps, better, it is to be understood as power to empower, not as power to dominate. To return to the story at the beginning of this chapter, recall that the two deacons enabled their peers to become "deacons" to each other, to their spouses and to their children. Their world changed because of the diakonia of two deacons.

The outstanding deacons, both before and after ordination, seem to be the ones who recognize and respond to their call to be of service. We wish now to reflect on their response in the context of a virtue which has been traditional in Catholic circles but which, we believe, has not been understood in its depth. That virtue is the virtue of evangelical poverty.

As he was leaving the church after his ordination a great deacon whom we know said something wonderfully insightful: "Now I no longer live on my time." It expressed exactly, first of all, how he had exercised his diakonia prior to ordination and, secondly, how he understood his ordained diaconate. Diakonia, service, ministry, for him, was total availability to others, whether he was ordained or not. Ordination affirmed and reinforced that charism and that talent for availability to others, and placed it publicly at the disposal of the Church and of the Christ whom it serves. After careful consideration, we have decided that talent-charism is to be named *poverty* and is a primary charism required of a deacon.

"Blessed are you poor, for yours is the kingdom of God." Thus Luke opens his Sermon on the Plain (6:20). Matthew, on the other hand, prefers: "Blessed are the poor in spirit, for theirs is the kingdom of heaven" (5:3). The difference between the two is not without significance. The poor, in Luke's first century as in our twentieth century world, are those who lack any financial wealth and who, because of that, are socially weak, defenseless and powerless. Matthew's addition of "in spirit" moves the focus away, however, from simple economic poverty to the attitude that rules the poor person. The idea might be best expressed in the phrase "loyal to God," the intention being that financial poverty alone is useless unless the poor person is open to God in his life. One who is financially poor and damns God for his poverty is not exactly loyal to God, is not exactly ruled by God, and is certainly not in the kingdom of God. It is not financial poverty that is blessed but one's attitude to God within the context of one's poverty. The other side of the coin, of course, is just as true; it is not financial riches that blesses or damns a person, but the person's attitude to God in the midst of his riches. The attitude which Matthew sets in focus is social powerlessness coupled with an openness to God. It is that attitude, and not just economic poverty, which is true Gospel poverty, just as it was that attitude which was true poverty in the Old Testament and made one a member of God's loyal poor. It is precisely that quality of social powerlessness coupled with total openness to God that we have found over the years as a dominant theme among the outstanding deacons. It is that same quality we have found lacking in some way among the not-so-outstanding deacons.

Deacons are men of poverty. That does not mean necessarily that they are economically poor, though many of the outstanding ones we know fit in that category in America. No, it means rather that they are men who have chosen to be socially poor, socially powerless, men who have chosen to live no longer on their own time and under their own control but on other people's time and under other people's control. Above all it means that they are men who have chosen to live totally, and frighteningly, open to God and the demands he makes upon them as he presents himself to them incarnated in the poor and the sick and the imprisoned and the lepers of every kind in their society. The great Pauline hymn in the Letter to the Philippians tells us that Jesus "emptied himself, taking the form of a servant" (2:7). We have found that all the outstanding deacons for whom we have drawn a character composite have done the very same thing, namely, emptied themselves of power, position, status, control over their own lives, and given evidence of their talent for poverty long before their ordination.

In ordaining such men, the Church affirms their charism for poverty as its own and ordains them to exercise their talent on its behalf to build it up as the body of the Christ who emptied himself. That public and solemn affirmation of their talent for poverty has freed those who have had it and exercised it before ordination to become more and more poor in their lives, and has fitted them marvelously to wait, on behalf of the Church, on the tables of any lepers who present themselves to them.

The promise of the kind of poverty we have just elaborated is part of the Rite of Ordination to the Diaconate. The person to be ordained kneels before the bishop, places his hands inside the bishop's hands, and promises obedience to him and to his successors. We believe that the promise of obedience is, in reality, the promise of poverty as we have explained it. The action is the deacon's promise of poverty, his promise to live from now on entirely on the time of others. It is his promise to be socially powerless, as incarnation of both a Church called to powerlessness and a Christ who lived in powerlessness.

This chapter has been about incarnation: the incarnation of the glorified Jesus in the Church, and the incarnation of the Church in its ministers, in those who are baptized as well as in those who are also ordained. Ultimately, it has been about the symboling of the presence, the grace and the power of God in the presence, the gracious poverty, and the service of the Church's deacons. Some of the things we have said are in complete continuity with the ancient theological tradition; some of them are in continuity-discontinuity. However, we believe that the great Catholic tradition is not static and inert, but rather dynamic. If that were not so, the Jesus movement would never have left its Jewish origins. Loyalty to the Catholic tradition demands, not a sort of doctrinal fundamentalism, but an ongoing, living response to the call of God in his Christ to incarnate them anew in our ever-new experience. We believe that the modern permanent diaconate movement is a perfect parable of that, an obvious continuity that is in creative and tensive discontinuity with the ministerial element in the Catholic tradition. That is one of the realities that this book will seek to underscore. For we believe that it is a reality of great opportunity for the Church that is both the people of God and the diaconal body of Christ.

4.
What Is a Deacon?

This chapter will be about something of crucial importance for the well-being of the Church, namely, the selection of its ordained ministers. Throughout the years since the establishment of the permanent diaconate in this country, the question of selection has been a dominant one in the minds of directors of programs. "Who is a deacon?" they ask. "What is he about? How do we find him?" Now that we have completed our study of Church and have brought into focus the meaning of the deacon as sacramental symbol of the Church, several things become clear. One is the need for deacons who embody the charism of diakonia. Another is the need for a selection process to reveal such people so that we can ordain them deacons.

In 1978, the National Association of Permanent Diaconate Directors, consisting of many of the diocesan directors in the United States and Canada, entered into collaboration with Selection Research Incorporated (SRI), Lincoln, Nebraska. SRI has a long history of success in helping corporations and educational institutions choose personnel for positions varying from executives to secretaries, from teachers and administrators to support personnel on several levels. The company had created interviews for many of the human services, and just prior to 1978 had created a Perceiver Interview for Religious. The latter came about through the efforts of Sr. JoAnn Miller, O.S.F., who was working with SRI in the educational area of their business. The directors were inquiring about just such a selection instrument for deacons. After preliminary study indicated that SRI wanted very much to be of assistance, the Association hired SRI to do their study of outstanding deacons in this country as the first stage of creating the "Deacon Perceiver Interview."

SRI's normal method of approach was followed in the development of the Deacon Perceiver Interview. Those who would know were asked for the names of some forty deacons around the country who were considered by someone to be outstanding. The criterion was simple: "Who are the deacons you would like to have more of? Who are the ones who are having such an impact that you wish you could have many more like them?" Then Donald O. Clifton, the president of SRI, produced a likely set of questions to be answered by the "outstanding" after a focus group of deacons and directors described what they knew of "deacon." The live interview of the first forty "outstanding" produced answers, common answers in fact, to most of the questions. A comparison study was then made between the answers given by the "outstanding" group and by those who were good but not outstanding. The comparison showed that ordinary and outstanding people do not answer questions in the same way. Clifton and his associates, whose job it is to do such work, discovered "themes" of life that were common among the outstanding deacons. In every person there are "themes" that characterize his or her dominant behavior over a long period of time. These are recurring patterns of thought, feeling and behavior that can be aroused spontaneously and that can help explain a particular person's success.

In developing the Deacon Perceiver Interview Dr. Clifton identified the life themes of outstanding deacons, those themes that explain their success as deacons. He created an interview to assess those talents in already ordained deacons, and did the necessary validation research to assure that the interview measures what it says it will measure. The end result of the research is the Deacon Perceiver Interview, a nine-theme, fifty-four-question, face-to-face interview which helps identify most reliably the qualities found in the deacons we want more of. Those trained to use it know that the Interview allows the prepared mind to clearly see what deacon "talent" is present in an applicant. It is also excellent for the evaluation and the development of the candidate both before and after ordination.

Having been involved in the selection, formation, training, evaluation and call of deacon candidates since 1971, we authors are convinced that we have never "made" a deacon. Deacon talent is either there when training begins, or it will never be there. The Perceiver Interview uncovers clearly in advance whether that talent is or is not there, and is, in our minds, the most significant breakthrough in the discovering and development of deacon talent in America. The reason has to do with the selection process. When a person has the talent to be a deacon, he is a deacon wherever he is. He does not "need" functions, liturgical, sacramental, scriptural, official or unofficial, to *be* a deacon. He does not ask "What will I do as a deacon?" He *is* a deacon, a natural deacon, one who has a deacon nature on which grace can build. The Spirit of God has something special to work with in such a man, namely, a nature that is diaconal and which symbolizes in and for the Church the meaning of the diakonia to which it is called.

There are nine themes common to outstanding deacons, arranged in three groups of three. There are core themes, those which are essential to successful, sensitive, teaming ministry. There are motivational themes, those which move a deacon to use the core themes. There are value themes, which give meaning to a deacon's life. The core themes are called Helping, Teaming and Accommodating.

HELPING THEME.

A person strong in this theme is a highly sensitive, perceptive, and accepting person. He is attracted to another person who has a particular problem and then follows through in helping that person by being particularly sensitive to the person first, and to the problem second. This person is often active in helping others and will take risks psychologically or physically to benefit another.

TEAMING THEME.

A person strong in this theme works hard at building a team climate. He is affirming and group enhancing. He is active in support of other team members. He helps others work together effectively and with minimal conflict.

ACCOMMODATING THEME.

A person strong in this theme is always giving of himself to others. He is very generous with his time and his energy and he is highly flexible in responding to the needs and wishes of others. He seeks affirmation by being pleasing to others. He gives of himself ceaselessly without counting the cost.

Motivation of the outstanding deacons was found to be in themes that had to do with people. They spend time with people easily. They like to be liked by others. Good deacons are naturally very active men who prefer to be involved in activities that demand energy and action. The themes considered motivational in outstanding deacons are described as Relator, Positive Others' Perception and Purpose.

RELATOR THEME.

A person strong in this theme enjoys working with people and desires a personal, warm, positive relationship with other persons. He attempts to build trust with others and to get to know them on a personal, supportive level.

POSITIVE OTHERS' PERCEPTION THEME.

This theme is the basic derivative of a history of positive affirmation by others. From his earliest life, a person strong in this theme has seen himself as a self-giving, "good" person. He seeks affirmation by being pleasing to others, helping others, relating to others, and resolving conflicts for others. He desires others to see him as a good, helpful and dependable servant of others.

PURPOSE THEME.

A person strong in this theme has a strong belief system about the service that he has for others. He believes that his job is a calling. He desires to become a deacon because this will fulfill his need and institutionalize his servanthood. There is a focus emphasis in this particular theme in that he has been servant much of his life. His belief structure gives him a focus for such service.

Up to this point in the listing of themes, it is clear that one need not be Catholic or even Christian to qualify as outstanding deacon material. It is in the area of value system that the significant relationships with God, Jesus, Church and family enter into the picture.

SPIRITUALITY THEME.

A person strong in this theme draws upon his own sense of God and the Church to be helpful to others. He takes sound, psychological helpfulness and puts it into religious terms. This person takes seriously the Gospel command to "love one another as I have loved you." He has the faith that gives him the strength, confidence and peace that he needs to be consistent and helpful.

FAMILY THEME.

A person strong in this theme puts a high priority on family. Since early in life he has had close family relationships, and in adulthood such relationships continue. He believes that the marriage vows are sacred and binding. He also often integrates his family into his work in the Church or on the job.

In addition to the spirituality and family themes, the out-standing have strong drives to be very energetic and physically active people.

KINESTHETIC THEME.

A person strong in this theme has a high energy level. He needs little sleep and is always on the go. He likes to work and is active and involved in many different physical activities. He has a great deal of stamina and sees his activeness as a positive contribution to others. His belief structure gives him a focus of such service.

What we have described in these themes is the "outstand-ing" deacon, though we must be reasonable and realize that there is a range in "outstanding." In any selection process the trained person makes his or her own decision about where that range begins and ends. Our point is not the precise range of the outstanding, but that the talent described in and by the themes is present in our Church and is accessible to the trained ob-server. It needs to be invited by local churches to be presented to local bishops for ordination in the Church. The relationship of the deacon with the local church ought to be a natural and an obvious one.

In the last chapter, we stated that diakonia is an essential calling of the Church. That Church deserves the finest talent available to symbolize sacramentally not only itself as deacon, but also Jesus as primal deacon. As we shall see soon, every local church has an essential need for that spiritual leader called priest. What we are saying here is simply that it has an essential need also for that servant helper called deacon. In fact, it appears that any parish without the sacramental presence of a deacon to symbolize the call of the local church to diakonia is sacramentally incomplete. The themes answer a frequent question: Should a deacon be pastor of a parish? No, he should not. But any church with a pastor but no deacon is declaring in symbol the absence of diakonia from its mission. The themes uncover the relationship of a deacon and a priest; it is a relationship of helper to leader.

There are problems of interpretation, however, with the unexplained use of the words *helper* and *leader,* and so we must explain what we mean by them. To do that we offer this analogy. In a school there are many leadership roles. There is the overall leadership of the entire school which is exercised by the principal. There is also the classroom leadership which is exercised by each teacher. The teachers' leadership is necessary and significant, but its scope is more limited than that of the principal. In the overall picture of the school, there is no doubt that the principal is the leader and that the teachers are the helpers. So it is with priest and deacon. Both are necessary and significant; the leader cannot do it alone, and neither can the helper. In symbol and in sacrament both the priest and the deacon incarnate the Church on a local level; in everyday practicality also both are necessary.

Rather than simply assert all that, we propose now to demonstrate it by comparing priest themes to the deacon themes already presented. For, employing its normal methodology of studying the acknowledged outstanding, SRI has developed a configuration of themes for the outstanding priest. The Priest Perceiver Interview, completed only in 1983, has fourteen themes in the configuration of an outstanding priest.

Dr. Clifton, in his thirty years as a psychologist, has been interested in successful people and has studied thousands of them in a variety of professions. At the conclusion of the study which yielded the Priest Perceiver Interview, he stated: "Of all the great talent I have ever studied, no one has the capacity to touch deeply the lives of so many people as has the outstanding Catholic priest." When such a statement is set in the incarnational context in which this whole book is set, it becomes clear what it might mean that we get in touch with the presence of

God incarnated in his outstanding ministers. To clarify the distinction of priest and deacon, we shall list now the priest themes. Priest and deacon are not interchangeable roles in the Church. They are two quite distinct sacramental roles, requiring two very distinct talents. The deacon has been seen as the low focus helper. The priest is here seen as the leader who will provide the complementary high focus he needs.

The Priest Perceiver Interview defines in an organized way the answers to three sets of questions. First, can the person *do* priesthood? Second, if he can do it, *will* he do it? And finally, if he can and will do it, *how* will he do it? The "can do" themes describe the spiritual leader.

PRESENCE THEME.

This theme belongs to those who are regularly and almost spontaneously conscious of God's presence, of his beneficent action that affects the priest's own life and the lives of others. Sensing this presence, the priest experiences a continual response to God. This theme specifies the priest and affords him an opportunity to help other people see God's beneficent presence in ordinary experiences. This may be the critical theme of the priest, and it may function at its highest level only when it is also accompanied by a very strong relator theme. Such a priest very probably sensed God's action in his own life very early. His perception of it may have been so gradual, yet so persistent, that he was not aware of having been called at any particular time of life.

RELATOR THEME.

The relator desires positive personal relationships with others and has strategies to build them. Positive human relationships can extend from the minimum level of simple acceptance and recognition of another's worth as a human being to an active willingness to sacrifice one's life for another. The priest-relator moves easily beyond the minimum to seek an extended and enduring relationship of mutual support with others. From the effective priest's point of view, there appears to be no Christianity without positive relationships.

ENABLER THEME.

The enabler experiences satisfaction from observing each increment of growth in another person. Not only is the enabler attuned to noticing growth, but he also gives expression to his appreciation of that growth and becomes involved in assisting still further development. The enabling priest frees people for growth by supporting, teaching and delegating. He takes every opportunity to help parishioners understand the meaning of their experience. He searches with them to identify the choices available to them, respects their needs to make and take ownership of decisions and, by supporting their struggle to do so, sets them up for success.

EMPATHY THEME.

Empathy is the capacity for using subtle clues to sense or read the feelings of another. The knowledge of the emotions of another person may be used to plan how to develop a trusting relationship or may be used to manipulate that person. Other themes determine how the empathy will be used. The priest with high empathy can often sense and describe feelings of another person before that other can. However, the most effective priest would use his empathy to determine the readiness of a person to clarify and disclose feelings.

COURAGE THEME.

Courage is the capacity for asking others to make commitments. In the face of resistance, a courageous priest will only increase his determination. He is able to give voice to important and relevant ideas, but without becoming angry. He has the capacity to be direct and straightforward with people, to take charge, to give directions when necessary. He is ready to meet with people in very difficult times in their lives, and at those times he is able to call to their attention their talents and their opportunities for growth.

Will the person who has these core themes necessary for priesthood be a priest? Without the motivation, what we call the "will do" themes, he may not.

MISSION THEME.

The mission theme is that which takes some individuals and groups out of society's mainstream in order to preserve the quality and clarity of purpose of that mainstream. Anyone who possesses this theme perceives a significance in doing a task that transcends the task itself. By giving expression to this larger significance, the mission-oriented priest helps his parishioners sense the purpose of their own lives. For the priest, mission is other-centered, which means that his life should be spent for the development of others, especially for the development of the spiritual lives of others.

HOPE THEME.

The priest with this theme envisions the future with great optimism. He generates the feeling that the deepest human desires can be fulfilled. He helps people build visual images for their own careers and for the work of the Church. He generally nourishes the optimism of his parishioners and helps them be assured about eternal life.

LOYALTY THEME.

The loyalty theme involves the commitment and dedication of the priest to the Catholic Church. The loyal priest identifies with the tradition and history of the Catholic Church as others might identify with a nationality or a family. It is a forever relationship. Even in times of difficulty within the Church, he keeps in mind not only the problems, but also the past and the future of the Church.

COMMUNITY THEME.

The community theme reveals itself in the priest's shepherding of his parishioners, in his enhancing the way they feel about the parish and in his sensitivity to what they want. This theme leads the priest to stimulate fellowship and interaction among his parishioners, to build and to maintain feelings of belonging in these parishioners. Through the priest's stimulation, the parish becomes a support system for all its members.

EGO AWARENESS THEME.

If ego drive may be described as a person's drive to define his or her self as significant, then ego awareness is the person's capacity to identify the events, recognitions, achievements and feelings that lead to defining his or her self as significant. Persons with high ego awareness can be explicit about these definitions or significance. Although they may not always like all of their thoughts and feelings, priests can own them and, when appropriate, disclose them. Persons with low ego awareness are likely to deny personal feelings that they perceive as different from the norm, and such denial may interfere with their understanding of the feelings of others. Persons high in ego awareness, on the other hand, are most likely to be objective and, consequently, to be considered as trustworthy by associates.

If a person has the core talent and the necessary motivation for the priesthood, how will he do it? How will he accomplish it?

FOCUS THEME.

Focus is the capacity to take a direction and maintain it. The priest who possesses this theme is not only himself able to identify goals, actively pursue them and resist digression; he is also able to help his parishioners do the same. The priest with focus sets priorities, then selects activities to achieve these priorities in their order of importance. This theme includes also a persistence in pursuing goals that produce and project a sense of continuity and security. Absence of focus, on the other hand, results in a diffusion of energies, with many projects started but few, if any, carried through to completion.

ARRANGER THEME.

The arranger theme indicates a capacity for organizing persons, objects and settings in order to produce a desired impact. The priest is called to be an arranger in setting up meetings within the Church and in planning and conducting worship services. The effective arranger has an ability to anticipate and facilitate the groups' interaction. He is like a stage director. In the management of a parish, the arranger-priest is characterized by a tight/loose approach; he establishes a carefully crafted liturgy that will put his parishioners at ease in a structure within which they can experience decision-making, freedom and even tolerance for ambiguity.

OMNI THEME.

This theme is characteristic of one who believes in completeness and looks for completeness, but accepts the unanswered. The priest with the omni theme is stimulated by the unknown, formulates hypotheses about the unknown, may sometimes be perplexed about the unknown, yet is comfortable with it. This theme goes beyond the mere tolerance of ambiguity to the positive enjoyment of dealing with ambiguity. The priest with the omni theme may not always be able to offer specific alternative answers; rather he affirms that answers are to be discovered. He asks questions and relates experiences so that others may be encouraged toward adventure and discovery.

CONCEPTUAL THEME.

The conceptual theme is evident in the priest who can verbalize for his parishioners the meanings in Scripture and their own personal experiences. In this verbal ability he has both power and fluency. He is a ready learner who is continuously intrigued by experience and by the manner in which experience can be meaningful to himself and other people.

Ordination in the Church, as we shall see explicitly in the next chapter, ritually empowers ministers to be incarnations of the Church itself and also of its Christ; it publicly establishes them as other Christs. Both deacon and priest are such ministers in the Church incarnating diakonia, the one a helper-diakonia, the other a leader-diakonia. The more talented humanly each is for his job, the better incarnation will he present of an outstandingly human Christ. In the living out of the sacramental notion of Church, the priest-deacon relationship is a very significant one. To suggest, as some priests have done recently, that we do not need deacons because we have ministers of the Eucharist, lectors, and other lay ministers is to ignore the sacramental theology that is at the very heart of everything that is Catholic. That theology is thoroughly incarnational, seeing Jesus as the incarnation of God, the Church as the incarnation of Jesus, and ministers as the incarnation of the Church. For us to be Church is not just for us to carry out functions, as do extraordinary ministers, but it is for us as ministers to symbolize Church and thus also its Christ. It is all about *the* mark of the Catholic Church, namely, sacramentality.

The significance of the SRI process lies in its search for talent in the Church to be ordained deacon or priest. When we call to ordination men who do not have the talent to be priest or deacon—and it seems pointless to deny that sometimes that is what we do—we are creating problems both for those we ordain and for the Church in which we ordain them. Occasionally we hear a deacon, who has no great deacon talent, complain that some priest does not allow him to do any functions, or at least places serious limitations on his "functioning" as deacon. Our experience is that when outstanding deacon talent is present, a deacon does not need "functions" to identify himself as deacon. He is deacon wherever he is: at home as husband and father; at work as servant of all and as member of the team; in the neighborhood as helper to anyone in need. He *is* deacon. He does not *do* deacon. The outstanding deacon realizes that when liturgical functions are part of his diaconal role, he does them in function of his sacramental role to incarnate this Church's call to diakonia. On occasion a man with little deacon talent will give the impression of being a "super cleric," just as on occasion a man with little priest talent will give the same impression. Both conditions are very unfortunate. But neither need give rise to an outcry against ever again ordaining anyone.

Reflect for just a moment on how we have been selecting men for both offices. For the most part we wait for the Holy Spirit to announce to the person that he has a vocation and then we spend time and money on discerning whether he has any talent for either diaconate or priesthood. It seems to us to make much more sense that the Church should first seek out people with talent and then spend time and money to let grace build on nature. In that situation, training programs would be designed to discern the call of talented persons, rather than to discern the talent of called persons. The "problems" of relationships between priest and deacon would at least be minimized if care were taken in the selection process.

The future of the Church depends on the selection of the outstanding in it to sacramentalize both its ministry and that of its Christ. Outstanding priests and outstanding deacons do not threaten one another, nor are they threatened by outstanding lay people. For, since both are great enablers, they seek out outstanding talent to work side by side with them. A parish, which is a local incarnation of Church and of Jesus, is not sacramentally whole if it is without either priest or deacon.

This chapter sought to underscore two things in relation to that. First, that it is a matter of supreme importance for the wellbeing of our Church that both priests and deacons, sacraments of all our calls to ministry, be well chosen. Second, that there are now available instruments to ensure that they be so well chosen. It seems clear to us that the former will never happen until the latter are well understood and utilized.

5.
Ecclesial Ordination:
Marriage and Orders

Some years ago a married couple we know, extraordinary ministers of the Eucharist, used to visit each week the aged in a nursing home and bring them Communion. Recognizing their talent for diakonia, their local community affirmed it as its own talent and ordained the husband to the office of deacon to continue their diakonia on its behalf. After this ordination of the husband, the couple continued their ministry in the nursing home and expanded it to include a gathering of the patients at which the husband-deacon would give a little homily on some Gospel text and both would then offer Communion. That gathering required that the patients be brought from their rooms, many of them having to be wheeled in chairs by the deacon and his wife. One day, as she was being returned to her room by the wife, an old woman, who was quite deaf, asked this question: "Is he a priest?" The wife replied: "No, he's a deacon." That day the question was posed several times and the same answer was given. The next week the same question was asked several times and the same answer was given, and the next week and the next week. Finally, exasperated, one day the deacon's wife answered: "Yes, he's a priest," to which the old woman responded with some verve: "Then who are *you?*"

It is easy to see her real question and its source. Accustomed all her Catholic life to the ministry of celibate Catholic priests, she was puzzled by this ministry she now experienced in her nursing home, a ministry that was offered by a husband and a wife together. It is easy to imagine the flood of confusions in her not too lucid mind. How can this be, a husband and a wife ministering together? Are they Catholics at all or, maybe and understandably, are they a Protestant minister and his wife? And what am I doing by sharing in a Protestant ceremony which I have always heard is a grave sin? As long as she kept getting the answer, "No, he's a deacon," the flood was contained, since she didn't know what a deacon was. But once she heard, "Yes, he's a priest," the floodgates opened and her questions came pouring out. And they are all good questions, flowing out of an as-yet un-answered, perhaps even an as-yet unconfronted, series of radical questions. What precisely is a *married* permanent deacon? How is he different from a celibate transitional deacon (what an awful and grossly misleading phrase!) or a celibate permanent deacon? Does the fact that he is married make any difference to anything? How does his wife fit into his diaconate? What is the continuity, if any, between their unordained diaconate as couple and his now-ordained diaconate?

The questions pour out, not from some grand ivory tower theory, but from the lived experience of deacon-couples in North America. We believe it is time to, at least, start to face the questions and seek answers to them. We do not believe we have ab-solute answers yet, but we do believe we have beginning answers and that we have to make a start. We plan to do just that, and only that, in this chapter. And we plan to do it by first sketching a theology of ordination and a theology of Christian marriage, and then sketching points of mutual insertion between the two.

Every Catholic born since the Council of Trent in the six-teenth century has been able to answer the question: "How many sacraments are there?" The answer has been: "There are seven sacraments—baptism, confirmation, penance, Eucharist, ex-treme unction, holy orders and matrimony." Anyone who is still giving that answer to that question is now many years behind the Catholic times, for the contemporary Catholic answer to the question of how many sacraments is that there are nine; baptism, confirmation, reconciliation, Eucharist, anointing of the sick, diaconate, priesthood, episcopacy, and marriage. The big change is obvious. It is the breaking out of the one sacrament of holy orders into the three sacraments of diaconate, priesthood and episcopacy. Each of these is now regarded by the Catholic

Church as a quite different sacrament. All that concerns us here, though, is the sacrament of the holy order of diaconate.

In the terminology of contemporary sacramental theology, to say that diaconate is a sacrament is to say that it is a human action which is a symbol of the action of the Church, of Christ, and of God. It is a human action which reveals and makes real and celebrates an action of the Church, an action of Christ and an action of God. A big question at this point, of course, is what action of the Church, of Christ and of God is symboled by ordination. We would like to begin to tease out an answer to that question by reflecting on an ancient Christian way to speak of bishops and priests. They are said to be vicars of Christ, even other Christs. It is one thing, however, to assert that a priest is an "other Christ," and quite another thing to ground that assertion theologically. An analysis of what it might mean theologically will lead us into an understanding of the theology of the sacrament of orders.

The traditional ground for the statement that a priest is an other Christ has located it as a function of the power of orders. Because the priest has been ordained to apostolic office by a bishop who himself holds apostolic office, and who stands in a line going back to the apostles and, indeed, to Christ himself, he is a representative of Christ, an other Christ. This traditional insistence of an almost physical succession of ordination going back to Jesus himself has institutionalized the representative function of the priest. He is an other Christ because he directly represents Jesus the Christ. But it suffers from two serious drawbacks. First of all, the direct succession of contemporary bishops, and therefore also priests, in an unbroken line from Jesus is now regarded as seriously doubtful historically. Secondly, such a legitimation of the priest as an other Christ totally ignores the essential part played by the Church as an other Christ, indeed the body of Christ. There is another, more modern, approach which grounds the claim that the priest is an other Christ on the fact that he is directly a public representative of the Church and, therefore, indirectly, a representative of the Christ. Only because he is first a representative of the Church, the body of Christ, is the priest a representative of Christ.

We are now in a position to ask the two questions we began with in this section. First, in what sense is ordination a sacrament? Second, of what is it a sacrament? Our answer will be this. Ordination in the Church is a sacrament in the sense that it is a symbolic action. It proclaims, makes real, and celebrates the action of the Church. It affirms that this believer stands firmly in its tradition, and ordains him to be a public representative of the Church, of Christ whom the Church reveals, and of God whom Christ reveals. Ordination is a sacrament in the Church in which believers are designated as representatives of Christ and of God precisely insofar as, and to the extent that, they are faith-full representatives of the faith-full Church. We must now explain those assertions.

The Second Vatican Council speaks of several modes of Christ's presence in the Church. He is present "especially in its liturgical celebrations"; he is present in the Eucharist, both in the person of the minister and, especially, under the eucharistic species; he is present in the sacraments "by his power"; he is present in the word that is proclaimed; he is present in the praying Church. The preparatory schema for the document on the liturgy was much stronger theologically. It sought to establish an order in those presences, from Christ's abiding presence in the community of the faithful to his presence in word, prayer, sacrament and Eucharist. But that ordering effort could not win enough votes in the assembly to be passed, mostly because the majority of bishops present wished to give precedence to Christ's presence in the eucharistic minister (the vicar of Christ) and in the eucharistic species (the body of Christ).

Now the central message of the New Testament is that God

raised Jesus from the dead and revealed him as so raised to selected witnesses. It was this act of God raising Jesus from the
dead that established the objective presence of Jesus for men and
women. But that objective presence, to be personally real and
useful for them, needed to be drawn into personal presence. It
was drawn into personal presence by the faith of the first believers, who believed that God had raised Jesus and had made
him "Lord and Christ" (Acts 2:36). It was this faith in response
to God's mighty act of resurrection which brought into being the
community of faith called Church. It became the faith of this
community, the apostolic faith preserved in the great Catholic
Church, and shared with each local church. Apostolic ministry
and apostolic office is a ministry and an office to publicly witness
to that faith in the name of the Church, and by so doing shepherd
the Church to faith. Ordination in the Church establishes believers directly in a ministry and an office of diakonia to the faith
of the Church; it establishes them as vicars of the Church. It is
only to the extent that they are ordained as vicars of the faith-
full Church, which is the body of Christ, that they are ordained
also as vicars of Christ. Ordination is a sacramental action which
proclaims and makes real and celebrates the designation of this
believer as both a minister of the Church, that is, as one who
speaks and acts in its name, and, as a consequence of this designation by the Church, as a minister also of Christ and of God.
As always with sacraments, of course, a sacramental ceremony
needs to be followed by a life in accord with the ceremony to be
in any way fruitful.

What is it, then, that happens in the sacrament of diaconate? The ordaining bishop, the officially designated representative of the local church to the universal Church and of the
universal Church to the local church, lays his hands on each individual to be ordained and prays over them the prayer of ordination. "Lord, send forth upon them the Holy Spirit, that they
may be strengthened by the gift of your seven-fold grace to carry

out faithfully the work of the ministry. May they excel in every virtue: in love that is sincere, in concern for the sick and the poor, in unassuming authority, in self-discipline and in holiness of life. May their conduct exemplify your commandments and lead your people to imitate their purity of life. May they remain strong and steadfast in Christ, giving to the world the witness of a pure conscience. May they in this life imitate your Son who came, not to be served, but to serve."

This ordinary gesture of laying on hands and these ordinary words of prayer for the gift of the Holy Spirit are meaningful on several levels. They proclaim, make concretely real, and celebrate: (1) the public election of this believer from the apostolic Church and the public affirmation of his faith as the faith of this Church; (2) the public verification of his faith by the one who has both the charism and the office of guaranteeing the faith of this local church, namely, its bishop; (3) the public verification also of the presence of a talent and a charism for diakonia in him, which the Church affirms as the diakonia to which it is called by Christ and by God; (4) the ordination of this believer by the Church to a public ministry of diakonia in and on behalf of the Church, an ordination which affirms him as both a co-worker with the local bishop and a co-representative with him of the faith-full Church, both local and universal; (5) the ordination of this believer, therefore, as also a publicly designated minister of Christ, so that when he proclaims the Gospel, in word or in deed, when he serves the sick and the poor and the variously imprisoned and the countless lepers, it is the Church and Christ who proclaim the Gospels and who serve; (6) the authoritative proclamation of the presence of the gift of the Spirit of God in this believer and the invocation of this Spirit to grace him for diakonia; (7) the separation of this believer from the Church, to stand over against it as its head in diakonia; this separation is to be understood, however, as reinforcing his connection to the Church rather than as severing it, much as Christ as head is both connected to as well as separated from the Church. The candidate responds to it all: "I am ready and willing." It is his public statement of his acceptance of the Church's call and ordination to be its sacrament.

This election of the believer to be deacon, the verification in him of the charisms of apostolic faith and diakonia, his ordination in and by the Church, the proclamation of the Spirit of God in him, his separation from the Church—all are done by the Church in the bishop's laying on of hands and praying. But in and through those actions of the Church, they are done in symbol also by Christ and by God. It is precisely in that sense that the actions are symbol and sacrament. The election, the verification of faith, the ordination, the proclamation of the presence of the Spirit, the separation from the body of the Church—all of these are looked upon as permanent and, therefore, as not needing or even permitting repetition. It is precisely this permanence of all these elements that Catholic theology wished to underscore in the doctrine of the *character* which it assigned to the reception of the sacrament of orders.

That is, in brief outline, our theology of the sacrament of orders. We must now consider, again briefly, the sacrament of marriage. Religions of all kinds are always on the lookout for images of God and of his relationship to the men and women who believe in him. In the Old Testament we find an image, an action-image, which is known as the prophetic symbol. Jeremiah, for instance, buys an earthen pot, dashes it to the ground before a startled crowd, and proclaims the meaning of what he is doing. "Thus says the Lord of hosts: so will I break this people and this city, as one breaks a potter's vessel" (19:11). Ezekiel takes a sharp sword, shaves his hair with it, and divides it into three careful parts: one part he burns, another he scatters to the wind, and the third he carries around the city and shreds further with his sword. In prophetic explanation of his action he proclaims: "This is Jerusalem" (5:5). In the Acts of the Apostles, the prophet Agabus takes Paul's belt, binds his own hands and feet with it, and explains that "so shall the Jews at Jerusalem bind the man who owns this belt and deliver him into the hands of the Gentiles" (21:11).

Each prophet clarifies for his people the meaning of his action, which clarifies for us the meaning of a prophetic symbol. As Jeremiah shattered his pot, as Ezekiel cut and burned and shredded his hair, so God will shatter and burn and shred Jerusalem for its faithlessness. As Agabus bound his hands and feet, so the Jerusalem Jews will bind Paul's hands and feet and deliver him into captivity. The prophetic symbol is an action which represents something else. The meaning and the reality proclaimed and made concretely real in representation by Jeremiah is not the shattering of a cheap pot, but the shattering of Jerusalem. The prophetic symbol is a representative action, an action, that is, which proclaims and makes real some other, more fundamental reality precisely by representing it.

Now central to the Israelite understanding of their special relationship with God was the idea of their mutual convenant. Yahweh is the God of Israel, and Israel is the people of Yahweh, because Yahweh chose Israel to be, and Israel consented to be, his people. It is easy to predict that Israelites would seek a human image of their covenant-relationship with God. It is, perhaps, also easy to predict that the image they would select is that other mutual covenant called marriage, in which a man and woman mutually choose one another to be, and consent to be, husband and wife. Easy or not, that is the image they selected.

The marriage of the prophet Hosea and the woman Gomer is, to every superficial appraisal, just like many another marriage. But on a deeper level, it became a prophetic symbol, proclaiming, making real, and celebrating in representative image the covenant relationship between Yahweh and Israel. The names of Hosea's two younger children reflect the sad state of that relationship on Israel's part: a daughter is named "Not Pitied" (1:6), and a son "Not My People" (1:9). As Gomer left Hosea for another lover, it was proclaimed prophetically that so also did Israel leave Yahweh for other gods and become "Not My People" and "Not Pitied." But Hosea's remarkable reaction reveals and makes real and celebrates the equally remarkable reaction of Yahweh. He takes Gomer back; he loves her still "even as Yahweh loves the people of Israel, though they turn to other gods" (3:1). Hosea's human action is prophetic symbol, representative image, of God's divine action, a steadfast and unfailing loving of Israel. In both cases, that of the human marriage of Hosea and Gomer and of the divine marriage of Yahweh and Israel, the covenant relationship had been violated. But Hosea's action both represents and reveals Yahweh's steadfastness. It proclaims and makes real not only Hosea's faithfulness to the end, but also Yahweh's. As did Hosea, so also will Yahweh "have pity on Not Pitied" and "say to Not My People, 'You are my people.' " And they will say "Thou art my God" (2:23), and both covenants will be maintained.

What should we make of this marriage between Hosea and Gomer? One basic meaning about Hosea (and Yahweh) is clear: Hosea (and Yahweh) is faithful. But there is also a clear, if mysterious, meaning about marriage. Besides being a universal secular institution, it is also a prophetic symbol proclaiming and making real and celebrating in the world the steadfast, if somewhat shaky, union of Yahweh and his people. Lived into in this perspective, lived into in faith as we might say, marriage becomes a double-tiered reality. On one level, it bespeaks the mutual love of this man and this woman; on the other, this human love images and represents the mutual love of God and his people. First articulated by the prophet Hosea, this double-tiered view of human marriage becomes the Christian view of marriage that we find in the New Testament—with a slight twist.

The New Testament passage which presents marriage most clearly as a prophetic symbol is Ephesians 5:21–33. It occurs

within a larger context, which sets forth a list of household duties existing within a family of that time. The list is addressed
to wives (5:22), to husbands (5:25), to children (6:1), to slaves
(6:5), and to masters (6:9). What concerns us here, of course, is
what is said of the pair "wife-husband." The basic attitude that
should exist among Christians is stated in 5:21: "Be subject to
one another out of reverence for Christ." Mutual submission is
to be practiced by all Christians, by all who are filled with the
Spirit (5:18), because their absolutely basic attitude is that they
reverence Christ. If all Christians are to be mutually submissive,
then, of course, so too are Christian wives and husbands, and so
it is no surprise that a wife is immediately instructed to submit
to her husband, "as to the Lord" (5:22).

But there is a surprise in the text for the ingrained male
attitude that sees the husband as supreme lord and master of his
wife, and that appeals to Ephesians 5:22–23 to ground and sustain that attitude. The text does not read that "the husband is
the head of the wife" (which is the way it is usually read and
quoted), but rather that "the husband is the head of the wife in
the same way as Christ is head of the Church." A husband's
headship over his wife is in image of, and totally interpreted by,
Christ's headship over the Church. And that headship is une-
quivocally set forth in Mark 10:45: "The Son of Man came not
to be served but to serve, and to give his life." Service and the
giving of oneself is the Christ-way of being head, and Ephesians
testifies that it was in this way that "Christ loved the Church
and gave himself up for her" (5:25). A husband, therefore, is instructed to be head of his wife by submitting himself to her, by
serving her and by giving himself for her. The husband is to be
the first servant, the first deacon, of his wife.

Husbands are instructed to "love their wives as (= for they
are) their own bodies" (5:28). Throughout Ephesians the
Church is equated with the body of Christ (1:22–23; 2:14–16;
3:6; 4:4–16; 5:22–30). Love is always and essentially creative,

and the love of Christ brought forth the Church and made its members "members of his body" (5:30). In the same way, the mutual love of a husband and a wife creates such a unity between them that she may be called his body, and his love for her may be called love for his own body. But it is only within the creative love of marriage that the two become this one body. Prior to marriage, a man did not have this body, nor did a woman have this head. Each receives a gift in marriage, a complement neither had before, which so fulfills both of them that they are no longer two persons, but one.

Now the traditional biblical text which grounds all of this is Genesis 2:24, "They become one body." That classic Jewish statement is to be understood, of course, in its classic Jewish sense in which *body* and *person* are understood as identical. Becoming "one body," therefore, is to be understood in English as becoming "one person." Ephesians declares that "*this* is a great mystery" (5:32), and the Anchor Bible translation seeks to show that the mystery is that "this (passage) has an eminent secret meaning," which is that it refers to Christ and the Church. The author is well aware that this is not the traditional meaning assigned to the text, and he states this forthrightly: "*I* mean in reference to Christ and the Church" (5:32). He acknowledges the traditional meaning of the text that husband and wife become one body in marriage; indeed in v. 33 he returns to and demands that husband and wife live up to that precise meaning. But he chooses also to go beyond that meaning to insinuate another. Not only does Genesis 2:24 refer to the mutual union of husband and wife in a human marriage, but it also refers to the mutual union of Christ and the Church. It is a small step to see a human marriage as a prophetic, representative symbol of the union between Christ and the Church. That means that human marriage is two-tiered. On one level, it proclaims and makes real and celebrates the mutual union of this man and this woman. On another level, this union proclaims and makes real and celebrates in representation the union between Christ and the Church, a union which provides an ideal model for Christian marriage and for how Christian spouses should conduct themselves one toward the other.

Christian marriage, then, is a prophetic symbol in the human world of the union between God and his people and between Christ and his Church. On one level, Christian marriage is just a human reality in which a man and a woman live into their mutual love. But on another level, it is more—much more. For as a Christian man and a Christian woman live into their mutual union, they seek also to reveal by imaging and representing the prior steadfast unions of God and his people and of Christ and his Church. A husband and a wife in any human marriage say to one another: "I love you." A Christian husband and a Christian wife in a Christian marriage say that, of course, but also more. They say: "I love you as God loves his people and as Christ loves his Church." That is one of the human things that makes Christian marriage a prophetic symbol or sacrament, a two-tiered reality which proclaims and makes real and celebrates not only the love of a man and a woman, but also the love of Christ and of God.

To say that Christian marriage is a prophetic symbol is to say the same thing that traditional Catholic theology affirms when it says that Christian marriage is a sacrament. Both statements mean that it is an outward action (in this case marrying) in and through which a Christian man and a Christian woman make a conscious response to the mysterious God who calls them in Christ, not only to "love one another" (1 Jn 3:11), but also to love him "because he first loved us" (1 Jn 4:19). The response to that Gospel call does not take place simply in a marriage ceremony, but rather it takes place over the long haul in a married life. To say that Christian marriage is a sacrament is to say, therefore, not only that the wedding ceremony is sacramental, but also that the married life of this couple is sacramental. It is the same, of course, for ordination and for all the sacraments in the Church. A sacramental ceremony initiates a sacramental life, and it is always the sacramental life following the ceremony that is crucial.

Now that we have outlined our theology of both the sacrament of diaconate and the sacrament of marriage, we are in a position to reflect on the two questions on which this chapter is focused. First, what does it mean that the modern diaconate is predominantly a *married* diaconate? Second, what is the relationship, if any, between marriage and orders in a married diaconate? What follows in this chapter is a reflection on both those questions.

As we look back on the past fifteen years and the norms which govern them, one thing jumps to mind immediately. For the vast majority of those ordained to the permanent diaconate in those years, marriage has come first. There have been those who have been unmarried when they were ordained, and they, of course, have assumed the obligation to remain forever unmarried. But for the vast majority marriage has come first and then ordination. And that is the first thing that is meant by saying that the contemporary diaconate is a *married* diaconate, namely, that in terms of time, marriage comes first for deacons and then ordination. But that, we think you will agree, is a very superficial connection. We need to look deeper than that superficiality.

Everything that we said above about the sacrament of marriage comes into play here. A man and a woman, who seriously wish to enter into a *Christian* marriage, wish to enter a marriage which proclaims and realizes not only their mutual love, but also the mutual love of Christ and the Church which is his body. A traditional theology of marriage states that in entering into this union the marrying couple minister the sacrament to one another, while the priest, who must be present for the marriage to be valid, is present only as an official witness. We believe that this view of the minister in the sacrament of marriage seriously underestimates the place of the Church in the ritual and demands, therefore, a closer look.

It goes without saying that the Church, which sees itself as the body of Christ and as the primary symbol of Christ in the world, will be very much interested in any other reality which it sees as also a symbol of Christ. It goes without saying, therefore, that it will be very, very interested in Christian marriage. That interest is evident throughout history; today it is embodied in some kind of marriage preparation course. The purpose of that course is to discover if the two people proposing to enter into marriage have the charism for, not just marriage, but specifically *Christian* marriage. If the Pre-Marriage Inventory (PMI)*et al.* uncover the gifts which Christian marriage demands, then the Church joyfully admits the couple to marriage and blesses it. If the PMI uncovers a lack of gifts for Christian marriage, and sometimes it does, then it sorrowfully denies admission to marriage. The entire pre-marriage procedure, and especially and predictably the denial of Christian marriage, has produced a lot of anger in the Church. But, if we consider the symbolisms at play, we will uncover the place of the Church in Christian marriage as one that is more than just a legal witness.

Christian marriage, remember, is not just any marriage in which a woman and a man live into and out of their mutual love. It is such a marriage, of course, but it is also more. It is a human union which is also image and representation of the unions of God and his people and of Christ and his Church. In Christian marriage a man and a woman are called, as we have seen, to be submissive one to the other, to be of service one to the other, to be the first servants of one another. It is not too much to say that in a Christian marriage a man and a woman are called to mutual diakonia, to say that they are called to be deacons one to the other. It is not surprising, nor is it sticking its nose in where it does not belong, that the Church, which is called to be deacon and which is imaged in marriage, is very much interested in whether it will be imaged as deacon well or badly in this marriage. It is not surprising, therefore, that it prudently inquires into the charisms and talents that these two people bring to marriage, and then judges whether they have the talents that will enable them to become one person and so represent well the union of Christ and Church. Based on this judgment of talent, it judges either that the two people may not or may be admitted to a Christian marriage. In the case of the latter judgment, in the person of its ordained representative, the Church will not only witness the marriage, but will also bless it and support it and ordain it for its own purposes. Those purposes are that in this marriage this Christian man and this Christian woman will cease to be two, will become one, and will be, therefore, a good image of the union of itself and Christ. Its presence, supporting and blessing and ordaining this marriage, we believe, makes the Church much more than a mere witness of the marriage; it makes it at least a co-minister with the marrying couple.

Here is what happens in a Christian marriage ceremony. The man and the woman proclaim and make real and celebrate in a ritual of the Church their desire to be married and be one in words such as these: "I, N., take you, N., to be my lawful husband (wife). I promise to be true to you in good times and in bad, in sickness and in health. I will love you and honor you all the days of my life." An ordained representative of the Church, a deacon or a priest, then prays for them: "Almighty God, hear our prayers for N. and N., who have come here today to be united in the sacrament of marriage. Increase their faith in you and in each other, and through them bless your church." These words and the gestures associated with them, pronounced and done before the Church solemnly gathered, are meaningful on many levels. They proclaim and make real and celebrate: (1) the intention of the couple to enter into not only a marriage, but also a specifically Christian marriage; (2) the public affirmation by the Church of the faith of these believers as the faith of the Church; (3) the public verification of this faith by the one who shares in the bishop's charism and office of guaranteeing the faith of this local church, namely, its ordained representative; (4) the public verification by the Church of also the charism and talent for mutual diakonia in these believers, a diakonia which it acknowledges as its own; (5) the public ordination (and we use the word quite deliberately) of these believers to use their charism for the building up of unity, not only in themselves and in their family, but also in the Church; (6) the public ordination of this married couple to be a prophetic image of both the Church (Vatican II calls the family "the domestic Church") and its union with Christ whose body it is; (7) the public translation of the couple into the holy state of matrimony in the Church.

The intention of this couple to enter into Christian marriage, the affirmation and the verification by the Church of their faith as matching its apostolic faith, the verification of their charism for loving diakonia, and their ordination to be prophetic symbol of the Church and of its union with Christ are all done in words and actions by both the couple and the Church. But in and through those words and actions they are done also in symbol by Christ and by God. The entry of the couple into marriage, the affirmation and verification of their faith, the verification of their talent for diakonia, their ordination—all of these are looked upon as permanent and, therefore, as not needing or permitting repetition during the couple's lifetime. Catholic theology has sought to underscore this permanence of marriage in its doctrine of the *indissolubility* of marriage.

All Christians entering specifically into a Christian marriage, then, are ordained to a mutual service aimed at their becoming one person. The Church, itself called to loving service in imitation of Christ, is very much interested in how they succeed in their diakonia. Indeed, the success of the couple in their marriage diakonia is intimately connected with their subsequent call to diaconate. For the accepted guidelines require that anyone being called to married diaconate must be one who has made a success of his Christian marriage. That is not a new requirement in the Church. Already in the Letters to both Timothy and Titus, there is stated the ancient rule that a man who aspires to the ministry and office of bishop must be a man who has made a success of his own marriage and his own family (1 Tim 3:1–7; Tit 1:6–8). The modern rule for admission to the diaconate is that ancient Church rule applied to the ministry and office of deacon. It is as if the Church, in calling a successfully married man to the diaconate, is saying: we have seen your talent for diakonia in your marriage; we have seen how successful you have been at it; we are calling you now and ordaining you to expand it in and on behalf of the Church. For married deacons marriage comes first, not only superficially in terms of time, but also in terms of diaconal ministry. Since his marriage precedes his ordination, then, in his married diaconate his diakonia within the marriage will continue to hold priority over his diakonia within the larger Church. Married deacons need to be reminded about this priority, for the tensions created in the struggle between time given to marriage and time given to diaconate are a source of ongoing problems for many of them.

There is another tension-creating ambiguity involved in ordaining married men to the diaconate. In marriage the Church ordains two believers to become one person, reinforcing their call to unity by proclaiming that powerful word of God: "What God has joined together let no man put asunder" (Mt 19:6). In ordination to the diaconate, the same Church affirms and verifies that the talent of these two for mutual diakonia is such that they have succeeded in becoming one, and then drives a wedge between their unity by ordaining the man to diaconate, but not the woman. This is not the beginning of a discussion of the ordination of women, for we do not believe that this is the place to raise the question of women's ordination. We do believe, though, given the stance we are taking in this book, a stance having to do with symbol and sacrament and incarnation, that there is still a serious question to be asked. For, if we are talking in the Church about a specifically *married* diaconate, and if in Christian marriage we are talking about two becoming one, and if we are talking about ordaining to the diaconate those who have made a success of becoming one, what is symboled by ordaining only one of the two to diaconate?

We opened this chapter with a story about a good marriage, one in which two people served one another, became one, and then went out to serve together as one in the greater local church. Recognizing *their* talent for and success at diakonia, both in marriage and in the Church, the Church called *him* to ordination to the diaconate. Recall here the sacramental symbolisms involved in such ordination: the call of believers to be deacons, the affirmation and verification of their faith and their charism for diakonia, their ordination by the Church, their separation from and their still-connectedness to the Church. In the case of the couple in our story, the charism for diakonia was found in both partners in their marriage and also in their SRI profile. If the Church can affirm and ordain the talent of the husband in this case, we believe that it can and should affirm and ordain the talent of the wife. But if the Church cannot yet see its way clearly to ordain this woman to diaconate, we ask it to see its way to, at least, affirm in some rite her talent for diakonia as a talent of inestimable value to the Church. That it can easily do and ought in all logic to do.

In 1971 the United States Bishops' Committee on the Permanent Diaconate issued Guidelines for the formation and ministry of permanent deacons. Those Guidelines stated that it is necessary "to offer developmental programs for the wives, so that they too might be involved in personal growth experiences similar to those their husbands are undergoing. During a two-year program, candidates have unusual opportunities for personal growth. Unless their wives have a similar opportunity, there can be an imbalance that might affect the marital relationship" (n. 129). Those words proved wonderfully prophetic. For, in the early years of the contemporary diaconate, candidates did have unusual opportunities to grow, and many of them did grow unusually fast. Unfortunately, they grew much faster than their wives who were not involved in their deacon program, and the imbalance that resulted did affect the marital relationship mightily. This moved many program directors to try to involve wives in their program somehow. The "somehow" varied from the weak invitation for wives to participate if they wanted to, to the strong requirement that wives must participate or their husbands could not participate. In our local program, after one year of creating growth-imbalance with a husbands-only program, we moved quickly to involve wives as intimately as possible in the program, requiring them to do everything that their husbands had to do in the training program, including taking the SRI inventory leading to a talent profile. Those profiles have been very interesting, showing in many cases that the outstanding deacon talent in many successful Christian marriages lay in the wives. We say as honestly as we can "in many cases," and not as loosely as we can "in every case"; for such is not the case. Our profiles show a wide range in deacon talent in both husbands and wives.

That we do not ordain every man who completes our training program is by both our choice and, after discussion of the talent profile, theirs. But that we do not ordain even those women with outstanding deacon talent who complete our program is, of course, neither our choice nor, in many cases, theirs. That choice is imposed upon us by the present structure, and sometimes creates a tension which can seriously affect a marital relationship. In effect, in some cases, it drives a wedge between the couples who have been so successful in becoming one in marriage and, at least in symbol, drives asunder what they and the Church and God have put together in marriage.

What is symbolized and incarnated in a married diaconate is something contradictory and illogical. In the sacrament of marriage—and remember that that means not only the wedding ceremony but also the wedded life—what is symbolized is two becoming one person to symbolize the union of Church and Christ. In the sacrament of ordination, which also means both ordination ceremony and ordained life, what is symbolized is the separation of unity in diakonia and the call of only the husband to ordained diakonia. In a celibate diaconate, of course, there is no problem. For marriage may symbolize one thing in the Church and ordination may symbolize quite another, and there is no contradiction in the symbolisms since each sacrament is celebrated by quite different people. But in the *married* diaconate, where each sacrament is celebrated by many of the same people, there is a serious problem in contradictory symbolisms. That, of course, may be an argument for recognizing the permanent diaconate for what we believe it to be, namely, something quite new in the Church and not something that is in total continuity with what we have long known as the transitional diaconate. It is an argument also for ordaining married deacon talent where it is found, whether it be in husbands alone or in wives alone or in both as one couple. But since, in our desire to be loyal to the universal Church, we cannot do that yet, we do not do it. However, we can and do do something.

As we have already argued, the Church which is the body of Christ, the primal deacon, is called to be deacon. Ordination to the diaconate recognizes deacons when it finds them, verifies that their diakonia is the very diakonia that the Church is called to, and ordains them to continue it publicly on behalf of the Church. For the present, some outstanding deacon talent cannot be so ordained. But it can, indeed must, be recognized and affirmed so that it can be enabled to grow. And that is what we do in our local community with all talent that we cannot ordain—

we affirm it in a rite of affirmation within our growing deacon church.

Prior to the ordination of men to the order and office of diaconate, which takes place in the Cathedral of Saint Cecilia, the deacon community gathers as a community-church. At that gathering the entire community lays hands on all those who have completed the diaconate training program that year, and affirms whatever talent is there as talent that the person is called to use in ministry on behalf of the Church. It may be wife-talent or husband-talent; it may be parent-talent; it may be job-talent; it may be listening-talent; it may be deacon-talent. But whatever talent it is, in the ritual laying on of hands, which is an action open to all kinds of meaning in the history of the Church, it is affirmed as being a gift that is there and as being a gift of the Spirit of Christ which is to be used for the building up of the body of Christ. Because this is very much a private ceremony in a small part of the local church, we do not pretend that it is ordination in the fullest meaning that that word has in the Church. But it is ordination, nonetheless, in the analogous sense that a charism is recognized, and the person having it is called forth and authorized to use it in and on behalf of the Catholic Church. It is, at least, a rite that affirms talent; it is, at least, a rite that treats married couples as one and leaves them one, even though their gifts might be different. It is a rite that might even be included in the rite of ordination to the married diaconate. For, however much it might have to be distinguished from the rite of full public ordination in the Church, it is a rite that does not put asunder what Church and God have joined together. It is a rite in the right direction.

We would like to conclude this chapter with a short meditation on symbol, sacrament and incarnation. In Chapter 2 we argued that in the symbol of his humanity Jesus of Nazareth incarnates the invisible God. In Chapter 3 we argued that in the symbol of the gathered believers, the Church incarnates a now-invisible Jesus. In this chapter we have argued that in the symbol of the ordained believer the Church creates another Christ, that is, directly incarnates itself, the body of Christ, and indirectly incarnates Jesus the Christ. A married diaconate takes people who in marriage have been successful at imaging the unity of Church and Christ and ordains them as other Christs. We believe that it is worth meditating on the insight, which some theologians now accept as a given, that the ordained minister is another Christ only in the sense and to the extent that he incarnates in representative symbol directly the Church. Now, if we are not mistaken, the Church is notoriously male and female, and, therefore, if it is to be symboled in an ordained order, it would appear logically and also theologically sound that it would be best symboled in an order which is a mixed male and female order.

The Christ that the Church incarnates is the glorified Christ, the Christ that is the first-born of a new race, the Christ that is not only head but also members, the Christ that is, as Paul says, the new *adam* (cf. 1 Cor 15:21–22; Rom 5:12–21). Now the first *adam,* so the Sacred Scriptures tell us, was male and female (cf. Gen 1:27 and, especially, 5:2). Jewish rabbis teach that when a man and a woman are joined in marriage they become as one complete human being; marriage makes them *adam.* Christian theologians teach that when a man and a woman are joined in Christian marriage, they are ordained to become one body, one person, to image the oneness of the body of Christ and Christ. We are suggesting that for the diaconate to yield truly other Christs, it ought to be as was and is *adam,* as was and is *Church,* the body of the new *adam,* namely, male and female. We make this suggestion with loyalty and respect, but also fully aware that what Karl Rahner called the "none too lucid argument" of the "Declaration on the Question of the Admission of Women to the Catholic Priesthood" does not even remotely apply to the question of the ordination of women to the permanent diaconate. We make the suggestion with hope, believing with Paul that in the Church "there is neither Jew nor Greek, there is neither slave nor free, there is neither male nor female; for [we] are all one person in Christ" (Gal 3:28). If a church which is male and female together incarnates one person in Christ, it is not unthinkable that ordination, which creates in symbol other Christs, could be the ordination of gifted males and females. Until that day comes we invite the greater Church to join us in affirming ministerial talent wherever it is found.

6.
Deacon Stories

Theology without experience and theory without practice can be meaningless. The previous chapters have dealt with a lot of theory, assertions and even opinions about holy orders. We wish to reassert that we believe what we have said about Jesus, Church, ministry, priesthood and diaconate. In this chapter we want to tell some stories from deacon practice which illustrate and support the theory. The stories are ordinary stories to those who told them to us. None of them were volunteered, and some of them were told reluctantly, because deacons often have tendencies to feel embarrassed talking about themselves. Some bad, or badly understood, moral theology informs them that relating stories of how the Jesus they know and love sets people free today through them is prideful and wrong—or something. They forget how Jesus sent the apostles out to heal the blind, the lame and the deaf, to drive out devils and to raise up the dead, and how he had them return to share their ministerial success stories—and, when they did, how they rejoiced with each other at what they had done. In a couple of cases they had been unable to cast out devils, which occasioned the instruction that some devils are driven out only with prayer and fasting. The deacon stories that follow are success stories which, we believe, will embody for the reader what we would characterize as good diaconate.

Our first story is about a deacon who happens to be a person with great teaching ability, though for the most part he is not academically prepared for ordinary schools. He spent about ten years, almost to the present, teaching in a state technical college. His subject was auto body mechanics. For most of us, that means he taught young men and women how to unbend fenders and rebuild bodies of cars after accidents. He considered those students the focus of his ministry as deacon, to give them both the knowledge of auto repair and the self-image of worthwhile human beings. He taught them a lot about justice toward accident victims and toward insurance companies. He taught them how to begin a business, and not to gouge anyone, even their competitors. Last year he had a chance to go into business for himself, and did. But some of his reputation for teaching went with him.

What most of us who drive cars do not know is that in recent years the steel manufacturers have perfected a process to make the frames and bodies of cars much lighter, and at the same time much stronger. The manufacturers of cars really have done some great things to protect people who might be in accidents. The framing is such that the heavy motor in the front end is sent down and away from the passengers in case of an accident. It is good to know that we are protected. However, the ordinary auto body mechanic does not know how to repair the frame after that first accident. If he or she would repair using the methods traditional in the past, the frame would appear to be all right, but in fact would have lost all its strength. In a second accident, the front end could easily end up in the front seat.

Deacon Larry knows all that. He knows how to repair a car frame after an accident so that the engine does not end up in the driver's lap. He knows also how to teach others to do it right. Presently he travels around the United States and Canada teaching technical school teachers and others how to repair the frames. That is his focus of diaconate!

What do we learn about diaconate in this story? Who is a deacon? What does a deacon do? Where is a deacon? How is a deacon? Why is a deacon? It so happens that Larry was one of the deacons studied when SRI produced the Deacon Profile. He has those themes listed in Chapter 4; he is a deacon. What does he do? He uses the special talents he has to bring people to life, whether in the classroom or in the front seat of a car in the midst of an accident. He stands for justice toward all sides. He calls people to claim their identity as worthwhile people, and to use their talent to make life better for everyone. He touches lives in ways that even he cannot imagine as his knowledge is passed around this continent. That is what a deacon does. Where is he a deacon? Wherever he is. How is he a deacon? By being his empathetic, sensitive self who wants to help people with all the talent he has, and by accommodating the special need of the present day in the auto body repair department. But does he have to be a deacon to do all that? No, he does not. But he is a deacon, and he does it as a deacon. And that speaks to a large segment of the Church about using their talent to the utmost to protect and save lives. Because he is who he is, he serves wherever he is. And that, for us who care about sacraments, ought to be enough!

Our next story is about a deacon who works on the railroad lines as a foreman. He had worked in the same shop with approximately the same group of men for some ten years. Recently the supervisor of the group was sick for a prolonged period, and Deacon Jim was assigned the task of temporary supervisor. Now Jim is an extremely empathetic man, naturally in touch with the feelings of people. One thing he was sure of centered around one of the foremen: he was not a good leader of men. The supervisors always assigned this man to the most difficult situations, apparently hoping he would fail and quit the job, leaving everyone happy. With his empathy fully operational, Jim thought: "That foreman needs a victory." He went to two self-starters in the group, whom he knew would keep his confidence, and told them of his conclusion. He asked them if they would consider being two of the four man crew for the lengthy job ahead, and they agreed. In fact they didn't need a foreman, weak or strong. But they did their job, with two others, assigned by Deacon Jim. Management normally allotted the job 4,000 man-hours; the four men did it in about 2,200 hours. An Olympic victory!

That is not the end of the story. When a job takes considerably more or less than the allotted man-hours, the supervisor must write a report. Rarely are any affirmations given, but Jim had other plans. He wrote a letter of commendation about the foreman and the four men and, before he sealed it, he showed it to each of the five men, congratulated them and thanked them. The four men have since chosen to remain with the "bad" foreman, and the five continue to do magnificent work. Management, of course, is ecstatic about the man-hours saved, and even the foreman is happy.

The incarnation of Jesus at work through Deacon Jim in this story should be obvious enough. It is not outrageous to claim that before the incident is over we have six deacons at work. Not obvious, though, are the implications for the marriages of these men. To find at work meaningful relationships and creative activity that challenge a man to use all of his talents has to make for happier husbands and, therefore, happier homes. Again, Jim did not have to be an ordained deacon to do what he did. But, again, he is a deacon. We, who need tangible reminders of what it is to be a servant Church, can point to him as sacrament. And that is the great meaning of the story for us. Jim embodies what we believe about Church, about being the body of Christ. He sacramentalizes for us what the humanity of Jesus does at that railroad yard. For those of us who believe in sacraments, that is magnificent.

Our next deacon story was told to us initially as a failure story, not as a success story. Deacon John was asked to visit a high rise apartment building, housing a large number of elderly. He was to conduct both a service of the Word and a Communion service for the shut-ins who lived there. One of the folks who came regularly to the gathering was a woman in her seventies, a Catholic, who always refused to receive Communion. John is a very caring, sensitive person, and he spent a lot of his time talking to her privately. She confessed to him one day that in her late teens she had taken medicine to induce an abortion, and that ever since she had felt guilt, self-hatred, anxiety, fear, and rejection by the Church. Most of all, she "knew" she could not receive Holy Communion. All the best arguments John could muster were not enough to convince her of the possibility of reconciliation. Every week he would spend time with her, listening to her anger and pain, but she would never receive Holy Communion. Sad to tell, she died that way, apparently unreconciled to the Church.

That story was told to a group of men and women gathered to tell and listen to good deacon stories. John had to leave early to go sleep at the house that takes the overflow from a Catholic Worker-type center. However, the next day he came to us to tell the meaning of the story. He said, "I think the meaning of that story has to do with me, not with her." He explained how this elderly hurting woman drove him deeply into himself to ascertain what the Church was to him. Unwittingly, the Catholic Church had done all the things that were opposed to what he believed Jesus and the Church were about. Jesus sets people free, even from sins of abortion. Yet in her mind, this woman found the Church unforgiving, punishing, imprisoning. As the weeks of his ministry went by John realized that *he* was Church to her now, but in her pain she never really let him in, at least not to give her Holy Communion. One only need recall the story of the sower planting seed on the footpath! John told us that something serious happened to him when the woman died. He came to realize that he was called to be Church especially to the hurting. He began then to visit the jail weekly to listen to pain and to love the imprisoned. He's been doing that for many years now. Recently he has initiated a project which will house and feed street people in another part of the city. The great part of that is that he has introduced such need to many fellow parishioners who have been working in the project.

Reflection on this story leads to several possible conclusions. First, did he or didn't he give her "Communion"? We believe that he did indeed plant Jesus in her hurting heart, even if he did not get to place him in her mouth. He did it by loving her, by spending caring time with her. But, just as important, we believe that she revealed Jesus to him. "I was hungry and you gave me to eat." John learned to see a presence of Jesus in hurting people that few of us ever touch at all, let alone touch deeply. We believe, therefore, that this story tells of a classic case of "intercommunion." In his caring person, not in bread and wine, he brings her the body of Christ; in her hurting person, she brings him the same body. In their intercommunion with one another, each communes at last with their common Church and Lord and God. Of course, again, John did not have to be an ordained deacon to live out this story; this deacon has always been a great deacon. But, again, isn't it a wonder for us, who believe in sacraments as the embodiment of what we believe about God, Jesus and the Church, that John *is* a deacon and a sacrament for us?

A deacon couple told the following story. Their principal *diakonia* in their parish is helping folks grieve after the death of a loved one. The case they recounted involved the suicide of a fellow parishioner, about their age, with children who were classmates of their own children. When they received word from their priest about this death, they were crushed. Fortunately, the deacon-husband was home from work that day, and both Joe and his wife Mary went to the home of the grieving family. They spent several hours crying, listening, praying, wondering with the family—with all of the family, that is, except the dead man's father, who asked only casual questions which enabled him to avoid the whole situation. The couple began to help the family prepare the funeral liturgy. Again the father would not participate, nor would he on another visit the following day. It was only after the wake service, when everyone except the family, Joe, and Mary had gone, that he reached out his arms to her, hugged her, cried and said: "This [service] is the only good thing that has happened." The crying continued for some time. Mary cried again when she told us the story. We ought not to have to point out again that one does not have to be an ordained deacon to enable that father to come to grips with the death of his son. But isn't it gratifying to know that the Church is well served and well sacramentalized by outstanding deacons?

Our final story is told, not by a deacon, but by the recipient of a deacon's special sensitivity. The woman—we shall call her Betty—reported finding her husband dead of a shotgun blast in the basement of their home. She was arrested almost immediately and accused of murder; newspaper articles made it quite clear that she was guilty. The deacon, Steve, began a series of sessions with her on the day of her husband's death. Betty told us that her friends and family not only did not offer any support, but also joined in the outcry against her. Only Steve stayed with her, assuring her that if she had not committed murder, she would be found innocent. Mostly, she says, he was just with her, and she knew he was there. With the clouds of accusatory condemnation hanging over her, Betty found it particularly difficult to grieve over the loss of her husband. Even when investigation showed that she had not killed him, there loomed up another accusation that he had committed suicide. Through it all, Steve stood by her, allowing her to grieve in the midst of her terror. After many weeks of pain, loneliness, fear, and wonderment, the shooting was judged to have been accidental. Ask Betty if you want to know what deacons do; she will tell you how important they are. For the one person who stood by her for weeks on end was the deacon, Steve. Like Jesus, he gave her hope when all appeared to be lost. His persistent and consistent care kept her from despair. He was the one open door to life.

Again it is not essential that Steve be an ordained deacon to do what he did for Betty. But, again, the fact is that he *is* a deacon, and that he was the only one who stood by her, embodying for her the diakonia to which the Church is called. It was through him that she was able to touch God, even on the brink of disaster. What do deacons do? They do what Steve did. In their humanity they incarnate the Church, Jesus and God.

These stories, and many others, embody empathy, sensitivity, listening hearts, accommodation of people in need, redemptive love, hope, generosity, flexibility and commitment to the person of Jesus. In short they sacramentalize diakonia as we find it in the Church. Most good deacon stories could be told by unordained men and women who reflect on times in their lives when they were called out of themselves to plant themselves in love in the lives of others. That is what we are about as the baptized community of believers who have "put on Christ" (Gal 3:27). It is "natural" for the Christian to be servant because to be servant is the very mission of Jesus. Ordination to the holy order of diaconate does not place a person outside the ordinary, but simply establishes him as the public symbol of the diakonia to which we all are called in the Church that is the body of the deacon Christ.

7.

The Liturgical Role
of the Deacon

A young man arrived in a small town a few miles from Snake River Canyon. He approached the local hardware store to inquire about the availability of heavy duty cable, saying he wanted it to stretch across the canyon. The hardware owner asked why he wanted to do that, and was told "I want to walk across the canyon, and I prefer to do it on a wire!" The salesman's jaw dropped, but he went to look for the strongest wire he had. When the sale was completed, he asked the young man: "Just when do you intend to do this walk?" "In the morning, about ten o'clock," he was told.

That night the hardware man told a few of his friends about the young man and his plan. They all laughed in derision. But the next morning they went to the canyon and, sure enough, there was the young man putting the final touches on the wire. They watched as he took off his shoes, waved to them, and immediately proceeded to walk across the wire. Arriving safely on the other side, he turned, waved to them again, and then started on the return crossing. The small group was very affirming and gave him a great hand of applause. He said: "Did you like that? Tomorrow I will ride a bicycle across the canyon. Does anyone have one?" A youngster in the crowd offered him a bike, and he announced that he would ride it across the canyon at ten o'clock the next morning.

Everyone went home and spread the news about the young man and his courage. At ten the next morning a much larger crowd, including a local television crew, watched as the young man successfully rode his bike back and forth across the canyon. He again accepted their cheers and announced that the following morning he would repeat his bicycle ride across the canyon, but with a one hundred pound bag of grain on his back. Everyone cheered, for by now they believed that he could do almost anything. By the next morning, stands had been hastily erected, vendors were all over the area, and Howard Cosell had arrived with a full ABC color crew. Again the young man made his ride back and forth across the canyon to the wild cheers of the crowd. Cosell interviewed him and congratulated him, and on national television the young man announced that he was not finished yet. "Tomorrow, at ten in the morning, I shall ride my bike across the canyon with a man on my shoulders. But I shall need a volunteer." And above the noise of the crowd a voice said: "I am ready and willing." It was the voice of a man willing to have courage, to risk, to help with a necessary balance to entertain the crowd. The young man checked him out—thoroughly. The man on his shoulders better have good balance, a lot of courage, and some special talent if this show was ever to repeat!

Our story probably limps in places if one looks too closely, but it says a great deal to us about the seriousness of the relationship of the deacon and the priest in our Church. It suggests an experience of incarnation, an experience of the presence of God, incarnate in Jesus. The bike is the Church. The young man is the priest, out there somewhat alone, but with a lot of support from the affirming community. The priest needs a great deal of talent to lead the Church toward the kingdom. But it is a wondrous experience whenever he is able to let God peek through! Riding on his shoulders, after an "I am ready and willing," is another, the deacon, who is also talented, but in a different way from the priest. He is not in charge; the priest is. Together, with their different talents, they are to lead the Church into the kingdom. Both priest and deacon are public ministers going toward the kingdom; they enable the Church to do what they do when they go together.

In this chapter we want to look at that relationship from the standpoint of the liturgical role of the deacon, a role which is most often exercised not only in the company of the priest, but also in relationship to him. It is this liturgical role of the deacon that folks usually have in mind when they ask, "What do deacons do?" It is a role that we have not yet confronted, not because we believe it is unimportant, for we believe it is a mightily important dimension of the public nature of ordination. We have not dealt with it yet only because we were concerned that it be located in its proper context in a book on diaconate. And that proper context, we believe, is a context of *symbol,* not of function. We believe that the liturgical functions of a deacon have their significance in the symbolic nature of a deacon, or they have no specific significance at all. Our purpose in this chapter is to explore what the symbolism of ordained diaconate is.

When people ask "What do deacons do?" the expected answer is usually a liturgical one. Implied in the question are other ones. "Can he baptize? Can he hear confessions? Can he anoint the sick? Can he witness a marriage?" The question being asked is a *power* question. Now, it ought to be clear to the reader that in this book we are concerned with facets of ministry other than power. And to clarify the liturgical role of the ordained deacon, we will turn now to the rubrics of the Liturgy of the Word and the Liturgy of the Eucharist to see what functions the deacon carries out there. Our purpose is to try to clarify the deeper meaning of each of his functions.

The deacon carries the Book of the Gospels in the procession into the sanctuary. He brings the Word to be proclaimed in the Church into this local church. The ultimate meaning of this action is to be found in what he has been doing in the week since this church last solemnly gathered. During that week he has been carrying the Word he now carries into the assembly to work, to homes, to the sick and elderly, to the hurting, to those celebrating new life, to those anticipating entrance into eternal life. By this action, he not only proclaims to us that he has been doing that all week, but that we too have been, or at least should have been, doing it. And now we gather again, to hear proclaimed the Word that we have lived, which renews us and sends us forth to live it for another week.

In the rite of reconciliation, which opens the eucharistic celebration, the deacon invites the gathered church to be mindful of its failure to be one in love, to be aware of the disorder in its life, and especially to be aware of the poverty of its presence before God. The deacon theme called "Teaming," which we described above as the ordinary behavior of an authentic deacon, is sometimes expressed in this phrase, "The deacon is the glue of the community." Deacons are people who call others together in a positive team climate and enable them to work together in a team spirit. If that is what a deacon is, how apt it is that he would be the minister to call us to come together in a team spirit before the altar. His life, of course, should match his words, as the lives of all of us should match our words. His words inviting the gathered church to reconciliation should be mirrored in a life that embodies reconciliation.

The deacon proclaims the Gospel to the assembly of believers. He who is the sacramental expression of servant proclaims the message of the servant Jesus to those who believe in that Jesus. At his ordination, a ritual event of great importance to him and to the Church takes place. The bishop, in whom the whole Church is sacramentally symboled, hands him the Book of the Gospels, saying: "Receive the Gospel of Christ. Believe what you read. Teach what you believe. And practice what you teach." In these ritual words, the Church calls the deacon to be a person who has so consumed, and been consumed by, the good news that it transforms his life. It is precisely as such a sacramental good-news person that he stands before the gathered church to proclaim to it what has consumed him.

The deacon is called also to lead the church in the general intercessions. The presumption here is that the deacon is aware of the needs of the community, that he has his ears to the church's ground, and is therefore in a strong position to state its petitions. His empathy, one of the talents of an authentic deacon, places him constantly in positions which require him to listen. His role as the one who prays prayers of and for the faithful flows from and embodies his role of talented listener.

In the preparation of the gifts at the altar, the deacon has the task of preparing the chalice, placing the wine in it, and mixing a drop of water with the wine. This latter is a simple, but deeply meaningful, gesture. For what is to represent for us the blood of the covenant is now a mixture, a mixture of saints and sinners, of rich and poor, of men and women, of haves and have-nots, of powerful and powerless, all called together to be the people of the covenant, the body of Christ, the Church. That the water and the wine are fused into a unity by the action of the deacon symbolizes his position as the glue which helps to bind such a diverse body into a unity. Here again, as always, for those who have eyes to see, the simple gesture becomes a representative and deeply meaningful symbol.

The Vatican II Constitution on the Sacred Liturgy speaks clearly of the presence of Jesus in the minister at the altar (n. 7). It refers specifically, of course, to Jesus' presence in the Church's priest, and that is something that the Church needs to meditate on. But Jesus is sacramentally present also in the Church's other minister at the altar, namely, the Church's deacon, the helper, who stands at the presider's right hand. Together they embody sacramentally for the Church, not only the nature of the Church itself as called to service and leadership, but the very nature of the one who calls it, namely, Jesus, the primal leader and deacon. The Catholic Church has always insisted that the presence of God and Jesus within it needs to be represented sacramentally. It is not surprising, therefore, that it seeks to embody sacramentally in ordained ministers what it believes about Jesus. In sacramental symbolism, priest and deacon together proclaim and make real for the Church, not only the presence of Jesus, but also what the essential nature of that Jesus is. They represent for it that he is one who came not to be served but to serve, and remind it that as the body of this Jesus, the

Church is called to the same diakonia. The presence of the deacon at the altar is not for the sake of the deacon, but for the sake of the congregation. It is a presence which announces to it that the covenant to which it is called and which it remembers and celebrates here is a covenant which binds it to the service of the kingdom of God, not only in word but also in action.

Immediately after the words of institution in the eucharistic prayer, the deacon announces to the congregation: "Let us proclaim the mystery of faith." The congregation responds with the great paschal hymn: "Christ has died, Christ is risen, Christ will come again." It was in baptism that this Church first made that paschal proclamation, going down into the waters of death with Jesus, so that it could be raised with him to newness of life (cf. Rom 6:4). In his eucharistic invitation, the deacon is inviting the Church not only to proclaim this mystery again, but to see in him and in his diakonia for others a living incarnation of that mystery. It is as if he is saying to us: "If you want to know what it means to be plunged into the paschal mystery, watch me."

We recall here an unfortunate situation of a few years ago, when a deacon family experienced the trauma of having a daughter become pregnant prior to marriage. The family was a large one, and well known and well thought of. The pain was all the greater since they perceived themselves to be a "deacon family." Parishioners and friends, however, did not react in the expected way. They seemed, rather, really to identify with the family and their struggle, and to ask a basic question: "How do you continue to love your daughter in this circumstance?" That came to be the question the couple also asked themselves and their deacon community. They asked, in a sense, how to live the Easter mystery in this family context. And we would like every reader to know that when this deacon says "Watch me!" he really knows from experience what it means to rise from death to new life.

The deacon's next task is to announce to the congregation: "Let us offer to one another the sign of peace." Here he reminds the church that if we are truly in covenant with the God of peace and truly incarnation of the Prince of peace, we stand for peace: at home, at work, in our neighborhood, in our parish, in race relations, in the struggle for disarmament, on death row, in abortion clinics, in international relations, in feeding the hungry of the world. He invites us to offer signs of peace to those gathered with us in worship and unity, that the oneness of Christ celebrated and made real in Communion might fill our hearts. But again, as with his role as reconciler, the deacon invites us to peace only because he himself is a man of peace, and therefore an enabler of peace. His invitation to us is also a challenge to himself: "If you want to become a person of peace, watch me."

The deacon is an "ordinary minister of the Eucharist." That is a role of great sacramental significance. The Eucharist is the embodiment of the Church, the body of Christ, covenant meal, sacrifice, the bread of life, the presence of Jesus, ritual of reconciliation. If the deacon is an ordinary minister of all this, that means that the "ordinary minister of the Eucharist" has to do with much more than merely distributing Communion. In his role as ordinary minister, the deacon is called to bring Christ to people and to bring people to Christ. It is the Church that is called, and therefore all of us who are called, to do that. The deacon's role as ordinary minister of the Eucharist is both to invite us and to enable us to do it always. His final statement as ordinary minister is: "Let us go in peace to love and serve the Lord." That is his final invitation to "watch me," an invitation to the gathered church to follow him out, into homes and neighborhoods and workplaces, to be reconcilers, peacemakers, deacons, symbols of a servant Church and a servant Christ to the world.

When viewed in this thoroughly sacramental way, the role of the ordained deacon is seen to be a major one. It is limited to a few words and a few actions, all of which may appear to be insignificant. Some priests look upon the deacon's role as so insignificant that, even with a deacon present, they assume his role into theirs. That is very unfortunate for the Church. For we need all the symbols we can find to make real for us what it means to be another Christ in the world. The ordained deacon in his liturgical role, just as the ordained priest in his, is present at the Eucharist to symbolize the gathered congregation, and that is a vital role in the overall drama that is liturgical action. It should never be subsumed by another.

The deacon is an ordinary minister also of baptism. Again, his role can be understood as the role of a functionary who can officially pour water and say words which bring people into the Church, or it can be understood sacramentally to mean much more than that. Deacons by their very nature are people who invite and enable others to come into a community of faith. They are people in whom the Church has seen the new life of resurrection flourishing, and whom it has called to live that life officially on its behalf. It is wonderfully apt that they should be, with priests who are also talented and called, ordinary ministers of the ritual in which the Church celebrates death and resurrection. By his role as ordinary minister of baptism, the deacon proclaims and makes real and celebrates for the Church the entry of a new member into the body of Christ. He proclaims to the baptized, on behalf of the Church, "Watch me." Watch me if you would learn faith; watch me if you would learn love; watch me if you would learn diakonia; watch me if you would learn to be servant; watch me if you would learn to be worshiper; watch me if you would learn to be like Church and Jesus.

There is, of course, nothing magic in being baptized or in being ordained a deacon. What counts is not the baptism or the ordination ceremony, but the baptismal life and the ordained life that follows the ceremonies. It is such life that the deacon symbolizes for the Church, and therefore for the newly initiated member of the Church. An important ritual moment in the cer-

emony of baptism is the clothing of the newly baptized person in
"the white garment of Christ," as Cyprian of Carthage called it
in the third century. That white garment symbolizes a new person filled with the life of grace. That life is lived in relationship
with a God who has become incarnate in Jesus, who has become
incarnate in the Church into which a person is now baptized.
The deacon calls this Church to a nurturing relationship with
its new member, a warm human relationship in and through
which the newly baptized person will touch Church and Jesus
and God, and they will touch him or her. In symbol of this, the
deacon presents the person with a lighted candle, the light of
Christ. It is a promise that darkness and fear are expelled now
by light and embracing love. It is a promise once given by Jesus
to his disciples: "I am the light of the world." It is a promise now
given by another Christ, another light of the world, to a new
Christian, a new other Christ. It is also an invitation and a challenge to this new Christ, for it tells him or her: "You are the light
of the world."

The deacon is also an ordinary witness of marriage. As we
saw in the chapter on married diaconate, the role of married men
in ordained Catholic ministry is evolving. When the Church
calls a married man to ordination, he brings his married history
with him, and it will be evident as he ministers in public in the
Church. By calling him to ordained diaconate the Church has
affirmed both his talent for diakonia in the "domestic church"
and his success in it, and has ordained him to extend that diakonia publicly into the greater Church. At least twice in his
adult life, the deacon has made a solemn public commitment to
diakonia; once in his Christian marriage ritual, then again in his
ordination to the diaconate. He is present as the Church's representative witness at a marriage ceremony as one who has made
the same commitment the marrying couple are now making, and
as one who has made a success of it. He is present, that is, as

more than a legal witness, more than just a kind of justice of the peace. He is himself a sacrament, of both diaconal and married life, and it is precisely as such a sacrament that he not only witnesses to others' commitment, but also reveals to them what commitment means over a lifetime. He says yet again: "If you would learn Christian marriage, watch me." He not only witnesses Christian marriage, but he also ministers to it by being who he is, a successfully married deacon.

The deacon is an ordinary minister, finally, of Christian burial. It is no secret that death is difficult, not only for those who are dying but also, perhaps especially, for those who are left to grieve after a loved one has died. It is a time in life when outstanding empathetic, sympathetic, warm, loving, caring, humanity is required. The authentic deacon is a man of such talents whom the Church has ordained to diakonia of the grieving on its behalf. His diakonia here is not just to bury the dead, but to reveal to the grieving a hopeful life and to enable them to move toward it. It is not only that he is to do that on the Church's behalf, but also that he is to enable the Church—all of us—to live the very same warm, empathetic and loving diakonia.

We wish to call attention, finally, to a role of the deacon that has been the subject of a great deal of discussion, his role as minister of the Word. That role has raised frequently the question: Should deacons preach from the parish pulpit as priests do and, if so, with what kind of regularity? Our experience of deacons, supported by the themes of the outstanding discovered by the Deacon Perceiver Profile, indicates that the majority of deacons do not appear to have any special charism for pulpit preaching. Without question, they are called to proclaim the Gospel, at home, in the neighborhood, at work, in the social order, even on occasion to homilize. But the answer to the oft-asked question seems to us to be clear: those with a demonstrated talent for preaching should preach regularly from the parish pulpit; those without a demonstrated talent should not. That, of course, demands discernment of a charism, based on the talent of the individual deacon. Some situations call for a form of preaching quite different from oral preaching. The elderly, the sick, the imprisoned and the various types of lepers in our society need to hear words of love more than words of preaching; they need to receive the hugs of warm people more than their words of instruction.

The Deacon Perceiver Profile shows us that outstanding deacons are not a very reflective group, preferring action to thinking or meeting about it. They seem to do their best work on a one-to-one basis, with sensitive listening as their greatest ministerial strength. That type of person will not prepare easily a homily in the ordinary sense. He may take many hours to prepare it, hours that could have been used productively in what he is good at, namely, one-on-one ministry. This is not to deny the fact that there are deacons who do a great job of preaching. We repeat again. If the talent is there, use it; if it is not there, do not. While we recognize that the bishop gave the Book of Gospels to the deacon on ordination day, we do not read that gesture as meaning, necessarily, that he is to preach formally. Rather we read it as meaning that his life is to be a reflection of that Gospel. He is to preach always by his life, and in his words only if he has the talent for that. It is more important, for a Church that longs for models to emulate, to see good life-preaching than to hear bad oral-preaching.

In this chapter we have sought to situate the liturgical role of the deacon in a context of sacrament, not of functionary. We offer it for consideration, with the sincere hope that in the very near future deacons will be called forth from the community because they are what we have described them to be. The deacon's role is sacramental. Because he is sacrament of the Church, the gathered church needs to have a great deal to say about who is chosen to embody it. Our prayer is that deacons will be chosen because of their diaconal talents, which we believe are now measurable, and above all because of that talent which we have called poverty. That, we repeat, is their realization that they are not their own, but the Church's and the Lord's.

8.
What We Have Learned

*F*ourteen years of working with the selection, evaluation, education and formation of deacon candidates, deacons, and their wives has been one of the greatest graces ever offered to us. The motivation to serve God and his people, evident in the hundred or more couples who have invited us into their lives in deepest intimacy, has been a revelation to us. And we have learned much in that revelation, not just about human intimacy, but also about the Church we call Catholic. And that, too, has been to us a great grace.

In the earliest days of the restored diaconate in this country, we used to hear it said that the permanent diaconate would teach us what it means to be Church, would teach us about laity, about priest, even about episcopacy. We are willing to confess that we used to take the saying with a large grain of salt, but now we begin to see both that it is true and what it might mean. For while we know that we are far from having all the answers yet, and that we may, indeed, never have all of them, we know too that we have begun to find some of them. We know that outstanding deacons have taught us what diaconate is—not only what their diaconate is, but also what the diaconate of the whole Church is. At least that is true if, like us, you believe that deacons are sacraments. It is because we believe that, and because we hope for the Church, that we are impelled to share the information we have gathered from watching and listening to ordained deacons being symbols of diakonia in the Church. It is only faith that can both see, and see through, symbol. It is only faith that can see, and see through, deacon as symbol, to both the Church and the Jesus that are symbolized. But it was only faith that enabled the early Christians to see, and see through, Jesus as symbol to God. If anyone looks at ordained deacons without faith, then surely one will see only a functionary that is not necessary. We believe that completely. If we do not believe in sacrament when we call deacons to ordination, then surely we will see only an adjunct that is entirely unnecessary in our Church.

That might be the first great insight on which to meditate. Deacons not only *receive* the sacrament of holy orders, but also they *are* the sacrament! As in all sacraments, if we approach them without faith, they are quite meaningless. Just ask a non-believer about bread and wine, or water, or oil, or words. Sacraments are designed to make God and his Christ and his Church present, but only for those with faith. For those who lack faith, and for whom therefore the symbols are meaningless, bread and wine are an adequate meal, oil is greasy, water is wet, and words have a surface meaning. But for men and women of faith, they are the symbolic means of revealing and making real and celebrating the presence of other, deeper realities. So it is with the deacon. If we see him as nothing but a functionary, we have nothing but a functionary. If we see him as a threat to our power, then he is one who threatens our power. If we see him as a meaningless adjunct, then he is a meaningless adjunct. But—and this is a very important "but"—if we believe that those who are baptized into Christ have truly put on Christ, are truly more than may appear to casual inspection, then even a deacon might be something more than he appears to a very casual inspection. If we truly believe that we, the Church, are more than just a human gathering, are even the body of Christ called to diakonia and service, then we might see in faith that we need a concrete symbol to represent that dimension of ourselves as Church. If you have been reading carefully, then you will know already that we believe with the Church that the permanent deacon is that symbol, and that is the essence of both who he is and what he does.

Such a conclusion returns us to the source of our faith, the man Jesus of Nazareth. Most of us who grew up with a catechism in hand learned well that Jesus was God. We learned that so well that his humanity was, at least, overshadowed. He was a man who could do anything, because he was a man who was God, and God can do anything. So he touched lepers; so he healed the blind; so he cried in grief; so he planted himself in the lives of rejects and they were set free. He was God, and isn't it normal that he would do those things? But what have they to do with us? That is a radical question when it comes to ministry, for it is a question that asks what it means to minister. It is with a certain amount of difficulty that adult Catholics approach Jesus in his humanity. To some it verges on heresy to suggest that his humanity is really all we *can* see. Yet an appreciation of the humanity of Jesus is the key to understanding the ministry of Jesus. It is the key, indeed, to understanding all ministry today. For it was through that humanity that God was revealed to his people. It was a humanity so real, so free, so full, that the God who had become flesh in him could operate freely. Thereby we were redeemed.

The humanity of Jesus is encountered today in another sacrament, called the Church. And, wonder of wonders, that humanity is still filled with God. When the human beings in whom God dwells are as human as they can be, God still peeks through to reveal himself. But, again, faith is needed here. Without it we see only human beings and human actions. With it, we see God incarnated in humanity, or Jesus who incarnates him. Without faith, first century Palestinians saw a Jewish man who broke laws, caused trouble, confronted them, and spent time with sinners. With it, other first century Palestinians eventually saw through the man to God. Without faith, Jesus is just a man; without faith, the Church is just a gathering of people; without faith, any sacrament is just an everyday happening.

Continuing along this line of theological and sacramental thinking, the role of bishop takes on tremendous significance. At least it does when it is approached with faith. In the third century, St. Cyprian of Carthage, one of the great Fathers of the Church, said: "Where the bishop is, there is the Church." What a view through the window of faith. The bishop sacramentally embodies the Church and, therefore, Jesus. What an awesome responsibility for a mere man. Yet it makes sense to us. The Church, the body of Christ, is a very human community. Indeed, in its humanity, it allows the God dwelling at its heart to reveal himself to his people. It makes sense, therefore, that the responsibility of being bishop, of being the embodiment of Church and Christ, should rest in the one who has a clear talent for expressing the fully human dimensions of the reality called Church. And in that humanity, those of us with faith will see God peeking through. How great it is when we can say about our bishop: "It is as though God is with him all the time. It is as though God is in him." People said that about Jesus because his humanity was so real. He was not a worker of magic; he was a great lover. He was so fully human in his loving that people with faith could see God. So too the role of bishop calls for a great lover, a great human, in whom people of faith can discern the presence of God.

The "fact," if we can so degrade such a sacramental reality by calling it that, that the bishop is a sacrament of the full Christ is rooted in Church as the sacrament of Christ. The bishop is the leader of the Church on a diocesan level; the priest is the leader of the Church in a parish. The priest is called to be in a parish what the bishop is in a diocese. Both the bishop's and the priest's status as "an other Christ" has to find its most meaningful expression in the human qualities and talents of the man who is called to incarnate Jesus for the Church. It is not as though Jesus is not present in his Church; he is very much present. But his presence is not easily visible and palpable; it needs to be made palpable by being symbolized or, as we Catholics tend to say, sacramentalized. Jesus' authentic humanity revealed God present among his people. Priesthood calls for authentic humanity to do the same.

In summary of what we have been saying: faith is an essential virtue in the Christian tradition, not just to believe things but also to "see" them. We believe that faith is essential to see the humanity of Jesus at its depth as the revealer of God, and to see the Church at its depth as the revealer of Jesus. We believe that faith is just as necessary to see bishop, priest and deacon not only as those who have received the sacrament of holy orders, but also as those who are sacraments, of Church, of Christ, and of God. Christian faith finds both its expression and its celebration in such sacraments, which symbolize the meaning of the Church.

We believe that we now have an adequate answer to the question "What is a deacon?"—an answer rooted in both our theological theory and our experience over the years. A deacon is a sacrament or a symbol of what all the baptized in the Church are called to be. He is a deacon-servant ordained publicly by the Church not only to clarify, but also to enable, by his public life what all believers are called to be.

Clearly research such as that of Selection Research Incorporated has enabled us to describe the characteristics, or life themes, of effective and successful deacons. They are good relators who like to be good to and for others. They are empathetic listeners who care about people. They are high accommodators, easily able to live on other people's time and agenda. They are good team people, affirming and supportive of others. They are highly energetic, good family men, who have integrated their faith and spirituality into lives of service. The research shows us the "natural" deacon, or the qualities of life instinctive to a person who does in fact symbolize the servant role of diakonia in the Church. Knowing that "grace builds on nature," the expectations of deacons so selected are not superior to their capabilities. Such selection will, in the future, eliminate the problem recognized in some of those ordained who give appearances of an identification based too much on the externals of clerical status. Such selection will also eliminate frustration on the part of deacons who are not given functions proper to their office, since "natural" deacons do not need functions to find their identity as deacon. That is not to say that such a situation is entirely tolerable from every standpoint. It is to say only that it does not threaten the identity of the natural deacon. For those who are not natural deacons, but are ordained anyway, such a circumstance is a source of very great frustration.

Another insight for us centers around the question of what happens to the community when someone is ordained. Usually we ask what happens to the one ordained. But sacramentally it is just as significant to appreciate the community's experience of affirming and symbolizing itself in a person who represents diakonia for it. The focus then seems more correct, the focus being on the reality rather than on the symbol of the reality. Both are, of course, important and interrelated. But we seem to have forgotten the former in recent centuries by focusing so exclusively on the "power" of the latter. We have learned over the years that the diakonia which is symbolized is more important than the deacon who symbolizes it.

The description of priest themes from SRI helps clarify the distinction between priest and deacon thematically. We find it very helpful to clarify the relationship of the two offices as spiritual leader and spiritual helper. Talent is an essential ingredient for both offices, and for a good relationship between them. A weak leader and a strong helper can be in grave conflict, and so symbolize very badly the unity of the Church. A talented leader and a talented helper, on the other hand, form not only an effective team, but also a very effective symbol for the total Church. Those who complain stridently about the lack of great leaders among permanent deacons should pay particular attention to the deacon themes, which make quite clear that leadership is not a deacon talent, but a priest talent. It might help them to sort out the difference between a deacon and a priest, and to identify the proper talent for each office.

The need for the Church to choose its symbols carefully is now very clear to us. Good information about the talent needed to be priest, to be deacon, and to be bishop, allied with the courage to make a commitment to those with the talent, ensures that those ministers we choose would be symbols in the most gracefull way. History shows that sometimes we have ordained persons into the offices of deacon, priest and bishop without their possessing the necessary talent. Ordination institutionalizes the talent present in the Church. Talent comes first; institutionalizing it comes second. There is a saying, popular among the Scholastic philosophers: *Quidquid recipitur secundum modum recipientis recipitur.* It translates as: "Whatever is received is received according to the mode of the receiver." It paraphrases as: "When the Church ordains non-talented persons, the ordination is received by a non-talented person. Do not expect from him talented ministry." Such criticism is not stated lightly, or with irreverence. It is stated with a desire, a mission even, to call forth from the Church those persons who have the talents to proclaim the kingdom, to build up the body of Christ, to lead and to serve as did Jesus.

A deeper look into the themes of outstanding priests and deacons raises a question about the ordination of men as transitional deacons on the way to priesthood. What is the Church institutionalizing in this ordination? Is it the talent to be deacon? Or is it the talent to be priest? The SRI themes show quite clearly that those talents are not the same. Now if the time spent by transitional deacons is just a time of internship for priesthood, why does it need ordination? If ordination institutionalizes talent, does it make sense to institutionalize a transition? Internship for priesthood could be done without any specific sacramental celebration. We hear regularly that a lay person can do almost everything that an ordained deacon can do. Though the statement is aimed usually as an argument against the ordination of permanent deacons, it is a much more telling argument against the ordination of transitional deacons. We are saying that we see a need for a serious reassessment of the policy of ordaining transitional deacons, because the policy is perpetuating the institutionalization of contradictory symbols. We agree with historical theologian Michael Himes: the modern permanent diaconate is something new in the Church, and we should seek to create it new rather than look exclusively to the past for clues. Of this much we are quite certain: the institutionalization of the diakonia of both the permanent and the transitional deacon in the same ordination rite is ineffective symboling. At the very least, a new rite of diaconal ordination, which clarifies the difference between transitional and permanent ordination, is needed.

Diaconate is not essentially a functionary role. There are significant functions to be performed within it, but they are functions within a larger sacramental context. It is as such, and not as functions, that they are important for a sacramental Church. As was suggested earlier, a parish without a ministering deacon appears to us to be less than fully equipped sacramentally. For who embodies the call to diakonia in the parish? Do we want still in the contemporary Church to institutionalize the notion that the priest does it all? Or do priest and laity do it all? The problem with that approach in the Catholic tradition is that we believe in sacraments as our way of embodying what we are called to. And diaconate, not priesthood, is our way of sacramentally embodying our universal call to helping diakonia.

No major new revelation is involved when we say that women constitute approximately one-half of Church membership. Nor, given the sacramental approach we have taken throughout this book, will there be new revelation in the statement that this reality is badly reflected in the present structure. It is not our purpose to plead the case for the ordination to the priesthood of women with that spiritual-leader talent described by the priest themes. But, since we are offering a book on diaconate, we do wish to state our hope that soon a way will be found to ordain properly talented women to that sacramental office. We wish to restate also our belief, supported by both historical and theological precedent, that we see no absolute argument against their admission to that order.

In the context of the preceding paragraph, the present state of practice in the Catholic tradition raises some problems that need to be faced with sensitivity and faith. As stated in the body of this work, when both husband and wife have been outstanding examples of diakonia for the Church, they ought to be called to sacramentalize it for the larger Church. The Church celebrates the husband's call in his ordination to diaconate. It needs to find a creative way to celebrate the wife's call—a way that is affirming, a way that is public, so that she is not in his shadow. The ordination rite itself seems to us to be the place where that should be done.

The promise of obedience to the bishop in the ordination rite appears to us to be a ritual publicizing to the Church the deacon's vow of poverty. That vow may be the very root charism that is institutionalized in the rite. Most, we know, see that promise as putting the new deacon under the power of the bishop. We prefer to think of it as a ritualizing of the new deacon's commitment to the powerlessness of Jesus. We prefer to hear him stating: "Is there something I have that you need? If there is, you can have it." It is his very concrete statement of his willingness to be now on other people's time and to do the same "waiting on tables" that the first deacons did in the Acts of the Apostles. We believe that there is a talent for such poverty, to which Jesus calls us all, but we believe also that it is a talent that is not found in us all. Those called to ordination should certainly manifest the talent and the charism to exemplify it and to enable it in the Church. We believe that this poverty marks out a major area needing discernment during the stages of preparation for the priesthood and the diaconate. For it is not right, and it is not productive, to ask such poverty of those who do not have the talent for it.

The value of a community of men and women committed to a life of ordained ministry is in proportion to the love, strength and support it offers to each of them. God's way of dealing with his people in history has been a communal way. Our experience has taught us that a strong ministerial community provides an ongoing experience of incarnation. It is a source of dynamic ministry in those who continue to grow in it. The alternative is the "Lone Ranger" type of minister who must find renewed support in himself alone. Human experience in general, and our experience of deacon community in particular, make clear that loving community provides the healthiest environment in which to become human and to experience the ongoing incarnation of Jesus, and out of which to incarnate that Jesus for others.

A setting in which people can be free to share themselves, in joy and sadness, in hope and discouragement, in times of life and death, of success and failure, of prayer and aridity, begins to tap the possibilities of ministerial community. It is a setting in which incarnation can happen. The energizing qualities of a loving, intimate group of dedicated people is the base for grace-filled ministry to others. That community has the capacity to call deacon couples to share the life that is Jesus, whom they continue to experience with one another. It also provides an environment of rest for those who are burdened. To live community is not easy. It involves giving oneself away. But, as always, so also here, he who loses his life finds life in its fullness. It is in such a lost and found life, we believe, that Jesus is best incarnated for others.

Our experience is that diaconate formation programs reflect their directors. The theology, the direction, the meaning of the diaconate, the intimacy of community or lack of it, depend on the director. It makes sense, therefore, that the position of director be filled by a properly talented person, one with the ability to enable deacon men and women to be what they are called to be. Since diaconate is still a new creation, the director must be also a person of courage, willing to chart new frontiers of ministry. The director, in short, should possess a lot of the talent described in the priest themes, especially that talent called OMNI, that is, the searching for completeness allied to the capacity to live with incompleteness.

Deacon people are great human beings. They are empathetic, sensitive, helpful, generous, good relating people. A special problem most face might be called "ambiguity tolerance." The meaning of the phrase is a good deal more complex than its pronunciation. Deacons, remember, want to please everyone; that is part of their nature. But when they are called upon to do two or three things at the same time, each of the three things being the priority of someone other than the deacon, what are they to do then? What is the great accommodator to do? Well, usually he feels guilty, anxious, frustrated and inadequate. We wish to let all those great deacon personalities, ordained or not, know that it is a universal problem and that it has no simple solution. A good course in assertiveness training, a sensible spiritual director, an honest and loving spouse, the common sense to realize that no one can do everything at once—all these will help prevent burn-out. People with outstanding deacon talent need help to keep the talent, and themselves, in healthy, effective shape. For our purposes here we want people to know that they are pretty normal if they have those feelings of failure and guilt in not being able to please everyone. We ask them also not to be content to be their own directors in this matter, for it is always better to have help from someone who sees the larger picture a little more clearly.

Dreams and visions have been included in the above material. Our most faith-full dream is of a Church with leaders and helpers whose talent has been called forth to symbolize both the Church and its Christ. The selection of the properly talented in the Church for the important sacramental roles of bishop, priest and deacon ought to be the priority of the Church today. Outstanding people, those who have the talent, are already present in the Church. We need both the courage and the system to find the talent in our midst, to affirm it and to ordain it. We believe that a system which searches out and ordains talent will alleviate any numerical shortage of ordained ministers. We believe also that when talent is placed correctly the Church will truly be a sacramental reflection of the Jesus we find in the Gospels.

The only possible ending to this book is an expression of gratitude to all the great deacon people, men and women, who have brought us to know the diaconate. If it has not been clear up to this point, we wish to make it very clear now that we believe in the diaconate. We believe that as an institution it has already taught us, and will continue to teach the rest of the Church, about ourselves, our nature and our mission. We believe that as sacrament the deacon has the capacity to renew the vision the Church has of itself as a servant community, servant both to its own need to be set free in God's kingdom, and to the needs of a world that cries out to be set free. We believe all that because we have had the grace to know authentic deacons and to see their servant ministry. In and through them we have experienced the modern incarnation of God.

Appendix 1.

General Norms for Restoring the Permanent Diaconate in the Latin Church Pope Paul VI, June 18, 1967

Beginning already in the early days of the apostles, the Catholic Church has held in great veneration the sacred order of the diaconate, as the apostle to the Gentiles himself bears witness. He expressly sends his greeting to the deacons together with the bishops and instructs Timothy which virtues and qualities are to be sought in them in order that they may be regarded as worthy of their ministry.

Furthermore, the Second Ecumenical Vatican Council, following this very ancient tradition, made honorable mention of the diaconate in the Constitution which begins with the words "Lumen Gentium" where, after concerning itself with the bishops and the priests, it praised also the third rank of sacred orders, explaining its dignity and enumerating its functions.

Indeed while clearly recognizing on the one hand that "these functions very necessary to the life of the Church could in the present discipline of the Latin Church be carried out in many regions with difficulty," and while on the other hand wishing to make more suitable provision in a matter of such importance, the Council wisely decreed that the "diaconate in the future could be restored as a particular and permanent rank of the hierarchy."

Although some functions of the deacons, especially in missionary countries, are in fact accustomed to be entrusted to laymen, it is nevertheless "beneficial that those . . . who perform a truly diaconal ministry be strengthened by the imposition of hands, a tradition going back to the apostles, and be more closely joined to the altar so that they may more effectively carry out their ministry through the sacramental grace of the diaconate." Certainly in this way the special nature of this order will be shown most clearly. It is not to be considered as a mere step toward the priesthood, but it is so adorned with its own indelible character and its own special grace so that those who are called

131

to it "can permanently serve the mysteries of Christ and the Church."

Although the restoration of the permanent diaconate is not necessarily to be effected in the whole Latin Church since "it pertains to the competent territorial episcopal conferences, with the approval of the Supreme Pontiff, to decide whether and where it is timely that deacons of this kind be ordained for the care of souls," we therefore consider it not only proper but also necessary that specific and precise norms be given to adapt present discipline to the new precepts of the Ecumenical Council and to determine the proper conditions under which not only the ministry of the diaconate will be more advantageously regulated, but the training also of the candidates will be better suited to their different kinds of life, their common obligations and their sacred dignity.

Therefore, in the first place, all that is decreed in the Code of Canon Law about the rights and obligations of deacons, whether these rights and obligations be common to all clerics, or proper to deacons—all these, unless some other disposition has been made, we confirm and declare to be in force also for those who will remain permanently in the diaconate. In regard to these, we moreover decree the following.

1. It is the task of the legitimate assemblies of bishops or episcopal conferences to discuss, with the consent of the Supreme Pontiff whether and where—in view of the good of the faithful—the diaconate is be instituted as a proper and permanent rank of the hierarchy.
2. When asking the Apostolic See for approval, the reasons must be explained which favor the introduction of this new practice in a region as well as the circumstances which give well-founded hope of success. Likewise, the manner will have to be indicated in which the new discipline will be implemented, that is to say, whether it is a matter of conferring

the diaconate on "suitable young men for whom the law of celibacy must remain intact, or on men of more mature age, even upon those living in the married state," or on both kinds of candidates.

3. Once the approval of the Holy See has been obtained, it is within the powers of each ordinary, within the sphere of his own jurisdiction, to approve and ordain the candidates, unless special cases are concerned which exceed his faculties. Let the ordinaries, in drawing up the report on the state of their diocese, also mention this restored discipline.

4. By the law of the Church, confirmed by the Ecumenical Council itself, young men called to the diaconate are obliged to observe the law of celibacy.

5. The permanent diaconate may not be conferred before the completion of the twenty-fifth year. Nevertheless, an older age can be required by the episcopal conferences.

6. Let the young men to be trained for the diaconal office be received in a special institute where they will be put to the test and will be educated to live a truly evangelical life and prepared to fulfill usefully their own specific functions.

7. For the foundation of this institute, let the bishops of the same country or, if advantageous, of several countries, according to the diversity of circumstances, join their efforts. Let them choose, for its guidance, particularly suitable superiors and let them establish most accurate norms regarding discipline and the ordering of studies, observing the following prescriptions.

8. Let only those young men be admitted to training for the diaconate who have shown a natural inclination of the spirit to service of sacred hierarchy and of the Christian community and who have acquired a sufficiently good store of knowledge in keeping the custom of their people and country.

9. Specific training for the diaconate should be spread over a period of at least three years. The series of subjects, how-

ever, should be arranged in such a way that the candidates are ordinarily and gradually led to carrying out the various functions of the diaconate skillfully and beneficially. Moreover, the whole plan of studies can be so arranged that in the last year special training will be given for the various functions which deacons especially will carry out.

10. To this, moreover, should be added practice and training in teaching the elements of the Christian religion to children and other faithful, in familiarizing the people with sacred chant and in directing it, in reading the sacred books of Scripture at gatherings of the faithful, in addressing and exhorting the people, in administering the sacraments which pertain to them, in visiting the sick, and in general in fulfilling the ministries which can be entrusted to them.

11. Older men, whether single or married, can be called to the diaconate. The latter, however, are not to be admitted unless there is certainty not only about the wife's consent, but also about her blameless Christian life and those qualities which will neither impede nor bring dishonor on her husband's ministry.

12. The older age in this case is reached at the completion of the thirty-fifth year. Nevertheless, the age requirement is to be understood in this sense, namely, that no one can be called to the diaconate unless he has gained the high regard of the clergy and the faithful by a long example of truly Christian life, by his unexceptionable conduct, and by his ready disposition to be of service.

13. In the case of married men, care must be taken that only those are promoted to the diaconate who while living many years in matrimony have shown that they are ruling well their own household and who have a wife and children leading a truly Christian life and noted for their good reputation.

14. It is to be desired that such deacons be possessed of no small learning about which we have spoken in numbers 8, 9, 10

above, or that they at least be endowed with that knowledge which in the judgment of the episcopal conference is necessary for them to carry out their specific functions. Consequently, they are to be admitted for a time in a special school where they are to learn all that is necessary for worthily fulfilling the diaconal ministry.

15. Should this be impossible, let the candidate be entrusted for his education to an outstanding priest who will direct him and instruct him and be able to testify to his prudence and maturity. Care must always and emphatically be taken that only suitable and skilled men may be admitted to the sacred order.

16. Once they have received the order of deacon, even those who have been promoted at a more mature age, they cannot contract marriage by virtue of the traditional discipline of the Church.

17. Let care be taken that the deacons do not exercise an art or profession which in the judgment of the local ordinary is unfitting or impedes the fruitful exercise of the sacred office.

18. Any deacon who is not a professed member of a religious family must be duly enrolled in a diocese.

19. The norms in force with regard to caring for the fitting sustenance of priests and guaranteeing their social security are to be observed also in favor of the permanent deacons, taking into consideration also the family of married deacons and keeping article 21 of this letter in mind.

20. It is the function of the episcopal conference to issue definite norms on the proper sustenance of the deacon and his family in keeping with the various circumstances of place and time.

21. A deacon who exercises a civil profession must provide—to the extent in which it is possible—for his own needs and for those of his family with the proceeds of this profession.

22. According to the above-mentioned Constitution of the Sec-

ond Vatican Council it pertains to the deacon, to the extent that he has been authorized by the local ordinary, to attend to these functions: (1) to assist the bishop and the priest during liturgical actions in all things which the ritual of the different orders assign to him; (2) to administer baptism solemnly and to supply the ceremonies which may have been omitted when conferring it on children or adults; (3) to reserve the Eucharist and to distribute it to himself and to others, to bring it as Viaticum to the dying and to impart to the people benediction with the Blessed Sacrament with the sacred ciborium; (4) in the absence of a priest to assist at and to bless marriages in the name of Church by delegation from the bishop or pastor, observing the rest of the requirements which are in the Code of Canon Law, with Canon 1098 remaining firm and where what is said in regard to the priest is also to be understood in regard to the deacon; (5) to administer sacramentals and to officiate at funeral and burial services; (6) to read the sacred books of Scripture to the faithful and to instruct and exhort the people; (7) to preside at the worship and prayers of the people when a priest is not present; (8) to direct the liturgy of the word, particularly in the absence of a priest; (9) to carry out, in the name of the hierarchy, the duties of charity and of administration as well as works of social assistance; (10) to guide legitimately, in the name of the parish priest and of the bishop, remote Christian communities; (11) to promote and sustain the apostolic activities of laymen.

23. All these functions must be carried out in perfect communion with the bishop and with his presbytery, that is to say, under the authority of the bishop and of the priest who are in charge of the care of souls in that place.

24. Deacons, as much as possible, should have their part in pastoral councils.

25. Let the deacons, as those who serve the mysteries of Christ and of the Church, abstain from all vice and endeavor to be always pleasing to God, "ready for every good work" for the salvation of men. By reason, therefore, of the order received they must surpass by far all the others in the practice of liturgical life, in the love for prayer, in the divine service, in obedience, in charity, in chastity.

26. It will be the task of the episcopal conference to establish more efficacious norms to nourish the spiritual life of the deacons, both celibate and the married. Let the local ordinaries, however, see to it that all the deacons: (1) devote themselves assiduously to reading and meditating on the word of God; (2) frequently, and if possible every day, participate actively in the Sacrifice of the Mass, receive the sacrament of the Most Holy Eucharist and devoutly visit the Blessed Sacrament; (3) purify their souls frequently with the sacrament of penance and, for the purpose of receiving it worthily, examine their conscience each day; (4) venerate and love the Virgin Mary, the Mother of God, with fervent devotion.

27. It is a supremely fitting thing that permanent deacons recite every day at least part of the Divine Office, to be determined by the episcopal conference.

28. Diocesan deacons must, at least every third year, attend spiritual exercises in a religious house or pious institution designated by the ordinary.

29. Deacons are not to neglect studies, particularly the sacred ones; let them read assiduously the sacred books of Scripture; let them devote themselves to ecclesiastical studies in such a way that they can correctly explain Catholic teaching to the rest and become daily more capable of instructing and strengthening the minds of the faithful. For this purpose, let the deacons be called to meetings to be held at specified

times at which problems regarding their life and the sacred ministry are treated.

30. Because of the special character of the ministry entrusted to them they are bound to show reverence and obedience to the bishop; the bishops, however, should in the Lord highly esteem these ministers of the people of God and love them with the love of a father. If for just cause a deacon lives for a time outside his own diocese he should willingly submit to the supervision and authority of the local ordinary in those matters which pertain to the duties and functions of the diaconal state.

31. In the matter of wearing apparel the local custom will have to be observed according to the norms set down by the episcopal conference.

32. The institution of the permanent diaconate among religious is a right reserved to the Holy See which is exclusively competent to examine and approve the recommendations of the general chapters in the matter.

33. Let religious deacons exercise the diaconal ministry under the authority of the bishop and of their own superiors according to the norms in force for religious priests; they are also bound by the laws to which the members of the same religious family are obliged.

34. A religious deacon who lives either permanently or for a specified time in a region which lacks a permanent diaconate may not exercise diaconal functions except with the consent of the ordinary.

35. The provisions in nos. 32–34 regarding religious must be regarded as applying likewise to members of other institutes who profess the evangelical counsels.

36. Finally as regards the rite to be followed in conferring the sacred order of the diaconate and those orders which precede the diaconate, let the present discipline be observed until it is revised by the Holy See.

Finally, after issuing these norms the desire springs spontaneously from our heart that deacons in performing their arduous functions in the modern world follow the examples which we propose for their imitation—the example of St. Stephen the protomartyr, who as St. Irenaeus says "was the first chosen for diaconal service by the apostles," and of St. Lawrence of Rome "who was illustrious not only in the administration of the sacraments but also in the stewardship of the possessions of the Church."

We order, then, that what has been established by us in this letter, given *motu proprio,* be firm and valid, all things to the contrary notwithstanding.

Given at Rome, at St. Peter's on the feast of St. Ephrem the Syrian, June 18, 1967, in the fourth year of our pontificate.

Formal Request to Restore the Diaconate as a Permanent Order Presented to the Fathers of Vatican Council II in 1962 by the Original Deacon Circle, Munich, West Germany

*E*minentissime Domine,

The undersigned respectfully submit to their excellencies, the bishops of our Holy Mother the Church, the following considerations relative to the proposed restoration of the diaconate in accordance with the needs of the Church in our day.

1. Several times in the past four hundred years, notably at the Council of Trent and even more especially after the havoc of World War II, the question of restoring the diaconate has been discussed by both clergy and laity alike. On the level of practical action,' Catholic laymen—many of them married—have since 1951 devoted themselves to the work of the Church as catechists, teachers, social workers, etc. These men have formed what they call the "Diaconate Circle," in order to live and labor in the spirit of the diaconate, insofar as this is possible under present legislation. In the light and strength of faith they are endeavoring to prepare themselves for the office of the sacramental diaconate, in order to be ready if the Supreme Authority of the Church should see fit at some future time to call them to this office. Such groups, with priests as advisors, exist at present in Germany in the dioceses of Aschen, Cologne, Freiburg, Munich and Trier.

There is likewise an interest in the restoration of the diaconate in several religious congregations, such as the Benedictines, the Franciscans and the Rural Missionary Brothers (the "Freres Missionaries des Campagnes" in France). These envision having permanent ordained deacons, who would live a celibate life with religious vows. The task of these religious deacons would be to assist at the celebration of Holy Mass, such as was customary in the early Church, and to participate in the various apostolic and missionary works of the said congregations.

Bishops, priests and laymen from all parts of the world are

143

among those who favor the restoration of the diaconate and support the efforts of the above named groups. Moreover, articles have appeared on the subject in Catholic periodicals and publications in all the major languages of the world. Well-known theologians have studied the matter from the historical, theological and practical points of view, and have arrived at the consensus that the proposed restoration (1) is possible, (2) would bear great fruit in the interior life of the Church, and (3) would do much to foster the cause of unity among Christians which Christ so dearly desires. (The results of these studies are soon to be published in Germany under the title: "Diaconia in Christo. Uber die Erneuerung des Diakonates," edited by Father Karl Rahner, S.J. and Father Herbert Vorgrimler; Freiburg: Herder Publishing Company, 1962; 650 pages.) This question has also been treated by several of the individual preparatory commissions, as well as by the Central Preparatory Commission for the Second Vatican Council.

2. What are the essential features of the proposed restoration of the diaconate? The Church would ordain as permanent deacons men found to be called and suited to this office, including married men. By virtue of ordination these men would belong to the hierarchy of sacred orders in the Church as ministers of a lower rank, after the bishops and the priests. They would perform tasks proper to the restored diaconate: the work of assisting in the liturgy, the ministry of the word and offices of charity. These are tasks which do not necessarily require the power of priesthood, but which seem to require the grace bestowed by sacramental ordination. Thus they could fittingly be performed by ordained deacons.

3. Is there any basis for this project to be found in Scripture, tradition, theology and the history of the Church? The mission of the Church as bringer of Christ's salvation to men is primarily fulfilled through the sacraments. The sacraments ex-

ist for the sake of men (*sacramenta propter homines*). This is true also of holy orders, which is especially important in the economy of salvation because of its connection with the administration of the sacraments, particularly the sacrament of the Holy Eucharist. In addition to its orientation to the conferring of the sacraments, the sacrament of orders imposes the obligation of caring for souls. This necessarily implies a concern for the temporal needs of men, since material goods are in God's providence the necessary condition for living a decent human life and thus being able to pursue one's supernatural end. This fact brings a wide diversity into the apostolic work of the Church, requiring a great range of talents and capabilities, and making necessary a kind of "division of labor" among the Church's ordained ministers.

As far back as apostolic times it was realized that the duties of the ordained ministers of the Church are too many-sided to be performed by one type of minister alone. The apostles in the mother Church at Jerusalem saw clearly that they had received from the Lord the authority to differentiate the one sacramental hierarchical order into three distinct grades, each with its own proper function and dignity. They thus created the three distinct offices of bishop, priest and deacon, with the bishop's office possessing the fullness of the sacrament, and the priesthood and diaconate each participating in its own limited way in that fullness. In virtue of this authority received from Christ, the apostles appointed seven men for "service at the tables" (*ministrare mensis*—Acts 6:2). The seven were ordained for this office by prayer and the laying-on of hands (Acts 6:6), and were thus constituted a part of the ordained hierarchy of the Church.

In the New Testament writings, the deacons are closely associated with the bishops (cf. Phil 1:1; 1 Tim 3:8ff) and have as their special province the offices of charitable work. According to the certain and general teaching of theologians, the diaconate is a sacrament. This sacramentality was further emphasized by the Council of Trent, which declared the diaconate of divine institution (Denzinger 966), and by the Apostolic Constitution of Pope Pius XII, "Sacramentum ordinis" (Denzinger 2301).

The diaconate, to which, according to St. Paul (cf. 1 Tim 3:12), the earliest Church councils and the custom of the Eastern Churches up to the present day, married men are admitted, had in the early Church its own specific nature: the basic fundamental was always the liturgical office, while the exercise of the other essential offices, namely the works of charity and the ministry of the word, varied in importance according to the needs of particular places and times.

4. Why is such a restoration needed today? Reports on the pastoral situation throughout the world, plus actual apostolic experience, show that the works mentioned above, namely the administration of the sacraments plus the care of both the supernatural *and* temporal needs of souls, have multiplied and diversified to such a degree that they cannot be performed by the bishops and priests alone. Because of their dual nature, both temporal and supernatural, these works require specialized knowledge and intensive training, as well as the grace and authority which flow from sacramental ordination. Both these requirements would be met by the restoration of the diaconate in the manner described.

The tasks of the restored diaconate would all have their source and center in the intimate connection of the deacon's office with the Holy Eucharist. The specific function of the diaconate, however, is to "serve," as the word "deacon" itself implies and as the practice of the first deacons of the Church demonstrates (Acts 6:2). Would it not be a tremendous gain for the Church to have once again deacons, who would assist at the Holy Sacrifice of the Mass—especially in the *Missa cum diacono,* which was the original form of the Mass celebrated by a priest—by receiving the gifts of the people and distributing to the people in turn the sacred gift of the altar? Would it not further be a living testimony to the Church's concern for the temporal and supernatural welfare of men to have deacons engaged in actual charitable work, bringing not only the Eucharistic Bread but also the necessities of temporal life to the poor and suffering, bringing Christ both sacramentally and in his burning care for the lowly and oppressed into the places of neglect and destitution, of hunger and sickness? And would it not substantially relieve the often excessive burden of the priests and bishops to have deacons available who could impart religious instruction and, in cases of special aptitude, assume the task of preaching?

In mission countries and in lands suffering from a shortage of priests, the presence of deacons could prevent many infants from dying without the sacrament of baptism. In such situations, the deacon could also assist at weddings, preside at burial ceremonies, and perform other religious tasks which must often be omitted because of the rarity of a priest's visit. Especially on Sundays and holy days he could, in the absence of a priest, preside at divine worship with the people, conducting prayer services, giving religious instruction, preaching, and distributing Holy Communion. He could also bring the strength and comfort of the Eucharist to the sick and dying, in cases when it is impracticable for a priest to do so.

Not only in mission countries, but even in a normal parish situation the priests are frequently overworked. Their time and energy are often so taken up with parish duties, moderating parish organizations, instructing converts, teaching catechism, preparing candidates for first confession, First Communion, confirmation and marriage, etc., that their own interior life as well as personal spiritual and intellectual development must necessarily suffer. The presence of ordained deacons could greatly alleviate this situation, as they would be specially trained for the apostolic "service" mentioned above. In general, the center of their activity would always be the parish, but in specialized situations they could serve, for example, in outlying chapels not having a resident pastor, in Church-run homes and institutions, in apostolic work with specialized groups, etc. In addition to such parish assignments they could also be employed in projects of broader scope, on a diocesan or nationwide basis, as the varying needs of souls in different parts of the world would demand.

5. What position would the deacon occupy in the structure of the Church? He would have his own proper place and function as a distinctive member of the mystical body of Christ. His position as one who has been sacramentally ordained but is neither a priest nor a candidate for the priesthood would make him a kind of link between clergy and people. He would perform the tasks assigned by the bishop who had ordained him, thus freeing the priests for the tasks proper to the priesthood alone, and enabling the specific character of the priesthood to shine forth more clearly. His position would in no way infringe on the proper activity of the laymen in the Church, but would rather aid and support them in Catholic Action and other official apostolic works.

As a result, one could hope for a rejuvenation of the life of the parish and a new enrichment of the Church's care of souls. This would be of advantage for the universal Church, and need not in any way change the present course of training for the priesthood. The restored diaconate, with its own proper vocation, its own tasks and own course of training, could exist side by side with the institution of the diaconate as a stepping stone to the priesthood. As successors of the apostles, the bishops possess the power to confer the sacramental diaconate on men belonging to both these groups.

6. What of the question of celibacy? The celibacy of the priest plays an impressive part in witnessing to the reality of supernatural goods, especially in our day, when so much emphasis is placed on the goods of this world. This celibacy would also apply to deacons under the new plan, when they were members of religious orders. On the other hand, the Church is also stressing more and more today the witnessing power of the sacrament

of matrimony as a sign of Christ's union with his Church and as a means of sanctification in the world. As the diaconate of its nature does not require celibacy, it seems that there are rich potentialities for holiness in the married life for those who would also belong to the hierarchy of the Church as deacons. Moreover a married deacon would be especially qualified for many of the tasks and areas of apostolic activity mentioned above. The prayer life required of him would naturally have to correspond to his state of life as a married man and family head. The institution of married deacons thus presents great possibilities both for the sanctification of marriage and for the increased effectiveness of the Church's apostolate. Moreover, it seems that the institution of married deacons is essential to any successful restoration of the diaconate, such as is required by the needs of souls in our day.

7. What kind of man would be suitable for this office? He must be aware of the great dignity of his calling and filled with the spirit of selfless service of the Church and his fellow man. He must show the virtues of fraternal charity, simplicity, modesty and humility. He must have proven himself through his manner of life, his religious practice, his firmness and uprightness of character and his maturity. Insofar as the possibility of marriage is open to him, he must be determined to choose a spouse who shares his ideals and his dedication to the apostolate. If he is already married and is being considered for the diaconate, his conduct in his married and family life must also enter into the judgment as to his fitness for the office.

8. How would the project get started, if it were approved? In order to guarantee general unity of practice throughout the Church, certain fundamental principles and guidelines would have to be drawn up by the Supreme Authority of the Church. Then each individual ordinary, in conformity with the Holy See, could judge (1) whether the restoration of the diaconate is desirable and feasible in his diocese, (2) if so, exactly how the

guidelines of the Holy Father with regard to the training of candidates, etc., are to be locally implemented, and (3) what special tasks are to be assigned to the deacons in the particular diocese in question.

Moved by a firm faith in the sacramental grace and power of the diaconate, and acting in a spirit of reverential obedience towards their excellencies, the bishops of our Holy Mother the Church, the undersigned hereby respectfully request that the above suggestions be prayerfully considered, and that the described restoration of the diaconate be approved—at least in the nature of an experiment—by the fathers of the Second Vatican Council, assembled in unity with our reigning Supreme Pontiff, His Holiness Pope John XXIII.